To:

From:

Date:

EVERY WORD MATTERS

the key to a more intentional life

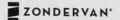

CAITLIN CROSBY

FOUNDER OF THE GIVING KEYS

ZONDERVAN

ZONDERVAN

Every Word Matters

© 2021 by Caitlin Crosby Benward

Requests for information should be addressed to:
Zondervan, *3900 Sparks Dr. SE, Grand Rapids, Michigan 49546*

ISBN 978-0-310-45463-2 (hardcover)
ISBN 978-0-310-45469-4 (eBook)
ISBN 978-0-310-45858-6 (audio)

Scripture quotations marked NIV are from the Holy Bible, New International Version®, NIV®. Copyright © 1973, 1978, 1984, 2011 by Biblica, Inc.® Used by permission of Zondervan. All rights reserved worldwide. www.zondervan.com. The "NIV" and "New International Version" are trademarks registered in the United States Patent and Trademark Office by Biblica, Inc.®

Any Internet addresses (websites, blogs, etc.) and telephone numbers in this book are offered as a resource. They are not intended in any way to be or imply an endorsement by Zondervan, nor does Zondervan vouch for the content of these sites and numbers for the life of this book.

The author is represented by Creative Arts Agency, 405 Lexington Avenue, 196 Floor, New York, NY 10174.

Photos © Emma Feil Photography and *Mini Magazine*: pages 83, 101
Photos © Moriah Smallbone: page 119
Photos © Virginia Kramer and Baby Henry Kramer: page 156

Cover Design: Tiffany Forrester
Cover Image: Tiffany Forrester
Interior Layout: Mallory Collins

Printed in India

21 22 23 24 25   BRI   10 9 8 7 6 5 4 3 2 1

Words have power. They are the building blocks of the stories we tell ourselves, the stories of who we are, what we do, and how we interact with the world. Those stories, and the words that make them up, matter. A single word can be the difference between a story of triumph and a story of failure. But the good news is that all of that power belongs to you. Your story is made up of the words you *choose* to use, the words you *choose* to believe about yourself, the words you *choose* to focus on and build your life around. If that's not empowering, then what is?

I'm Caitlin Crosby—wife to Colin; mama to my son, Brave, and my daughter, Love; CEO and founder of The Giving Keys; singer; songwriter; former actress; and human. As it turns out, I'm all about words. I've basically built my entire career on them—the words I said while acting in character, the words I wrote and then sang as a songwriter and musician. And the words I chose to engrave on an old beat-up hotel-key-turned-necklace that eventually launched The Giving Keys and led me to where I am today, a speaker and author who shares my words with others.

I have always wanted to do something that mattered, to be a force for positive change in the world, to be a part of something so much bigger than myself. A huge reason why I pursued acting and music was to create a platform to speak out about things I saw in the world (and in my own life) that broke my heart. Both of my parents worked in the entertainment industry, and growing up in Los Angeles with a small sliver of the world in front of me, it seemed like the best way to reach people was to become a big name. But what I've come to realize is that The Giving Keys was the exact answer to my prayer for a way to make a real difference. Turns out I didn't need fame and fortune—just a giving spirit, a dedication to our mission, a willingness to work hard, and an open heart.

If you are reading this book, then I know you feel it too—you want to make a difference in the world, in the lives of the people you love, or in your own life. No matter how difficult your path, how many obstacles you need to overcome, or just how exhausted you are, I firmly believe that we are all here for a reason. There is only one you in the entire world, and you have the power to write the incredible, inspiring, joyful story of your life with any words you choose. You have everything you need to create a deep, meaningful life and inspire everyone around you to do the same.

The idea for The Giving Keys started with Love Your Flawz, a movement I launched with fellow actress Brie Larson to encourage women to celebrate their so-called imperfections and love their unique bodies instead of constantly selling themselves short based on the unrealistic, cookie-cutter beauty standards set by magazines, movies, and the rest of the media. I released a solo album called *Flawz*, and while I was on tour promoting it, I would encourage everyone I met at my shows to make signs, saying things like:

My acne is beautiful.
My scar saved my life.
My cellulite is sexy.

These signs weren't exactly fancy. In fact, they were just scribbles on scraps of paper, but they were still powerful. The whole point was to pick new words for these beautiful women to help them change their stories, to help them rewrite the negative words they had believed about themselves for too long. Before I knew it, fans were posting pictures on social media with their own handmade signs. Choosing to own the words we use to describe ourselves is a powerful thing indeed.

A few years later, I was on another tour and staying in a hotel in New York City that gave out actual metal keys instead of key cards. It was so charming and authentic. I thought I'd lost my key, but a week or so later when we were far from New York, I found that lost key in my bag. Something about that key was so special. I'm not sure if it was how rusty and beat up it was, or just the thought of all the people who had used it that appealed to me, but I slipped it onto the necklace chain that I wore every day.

Back home, I was at a locksmith and realized they offered number engraving for apartments and the like. I immediately asked to have *Love Your Flawz* engraved on my banged-up hotel key. I loved the way it looked. While I was waiting, I noticed a bucket of discarded keys. The

We're all just walking each other home.

—RAM DASS

locksmith told me I could have them, and he'd engrave a word on each for eight dollars a key.

I had him engrave words like *hope, strength, courage, fight, believe, fearless, peace, dream,* and *faith.* Then I got to work, making jewelry to give to my family and friends. Everyone who received a key was deeply moved, so when it was time for me to go back out on tour, I decided to sell my key necklaces at each tour stop. The necklaces quickly became my biggest sellers. The same *something* about those keys that had resonated with me was making a big impact on the people attending the shows too.

Then one night, I had an idea that turned a simple key necklace into a pay-it-forward movement all its own. I told people to wear their keys until they met someone who needed the word on their necklace more than they did, and then give it away to that person. As fans did just that, my one-word keys blossomed into stories full of hope and inspiration and giving. The more of these stories I heard, the more I knew there needed to be a public place to share them, so I created TheGivingKeys. com, a simple website where people could share their experiences giving away their keys. Reading all of the stories that poured in convinced me that this movement could be so much bigger than tour merchandise.

I wanted to expand on the idea and build a store on The Giving Keys website, but the logistics of how to make it work felt overwhelming. How could I keep up with the demand of making each necklace by hand with my tweezers and nail clippers? Clearly, I did not have a sustainable business model! Luckily, the final piece of the puzzle slid into place one night after church when I met a couple named Rob and Cera, who were experiencing homelessness. I invited them to dinner, and when Cera mentioned she made her own jewelry, I felt like I'd been struck by a bolt of lightning. This was the answer! I hired them on the spot, ordered engraving kits and jewelry hammers, and got them to work engraving keys and turning them into necklaces. Over time we hired more and more workers, moved into an office, and today we've hired more than 130 people transitioning out of homelessness.

So that's the short version of my story. The long version is, of course, longer, but it's also full of more doubt, struggle, heartbreak, and shame. And I'm sure your long version is too—because, honestly, whose isn't? Perhaps you have an idea of how life is supposed to be, but not a single one of our stories *actually* follows our plans. Mostly, life is a series of colorful challenges and struggles, cringeworthy hiccups, teachable

Do not wait for leaders. Do it alone, person to person.

—MOTHER TERESA

failures, and big wins. But we always, always have a choice in how we tell the stories of our lives as we live them. We can choose to let our circumstances overwhelm us and keep us down, or we can choose to take those same circumstances and reframe them as chances to reach our full, beautiful potential. The words in our narratives are ours to craft. At the end of the day, I want my story to be one of healing, resilience, and strength. And I want that for you too.

People are always a little surprised at how excited I get when I pick out a new word to wear on a key, but the truth is I still need all of the words I've chosen for The Giving Keys. Words have power, and there is something *very* powerful about having a simple word carved into a metal key that you can wear, carry with you throughout your day, and run your fingers over in the dark. I think what resonated so much with me (and with everyone else who has purchased a Giving Key) is that we could all use a tangible reminder of the words we're working to write into our stories. Sometimes I pick a word because I need more of it in my life. Sometimes I pick a word as a reminder of a quality I already have. Sometimes I pick a word because it just feels right for the season I'm in.

Even if The Giving Keys went bust or I left the company to pursue a new dream (because change and new seasons are also beautiful), I would still pick out words to carry with me, to be inspired by, to draw strength and courage and comfort from. I'd write them on my hand, in my notebook, highlight them in books, text them to my friends, put them with hashtags on Instagram, and even scrawl them on the bathroom mirror in lipstick. Having a word helps focus my energy, my intentions, and my instincts. Having a word helps me keep on track for the goals I've set and the healing I'm working toward, and it helps me focus on my true priorities.

I think choosing a word can do the same for you. You don't need to buy a key necklace; you just have to choose a word that speaks to where you are, where you've been, and where you want to go. Let that word be a touchpoint to help you be intentional. Identify a word you know will be life-giving, and put more of that into your day-to-day life. Let your word seep down into your soul and radiate into every part of your story. If you are feeling weak, choose *strength* and push that strength into your relationships, choices, and self-talk. If you want to believe in something bigger than yourself, choose *faith*, and remember to believe in yourself as you make decisions, wrestle with dilemmas, and find peace amid the chaos. Starting a new career or side hustle? Choose *create* to remind yourself to keep going, even when it's difficult, even when it's ugly, until you create something beautiful.

We have to confront our fears, break free of our old, predictable patterns, and alter our perception so we can learn to see ourselves with new eyes. I'm getting there and so can you. Do you think you can use your word to pay closer attention to your body, your breath, your instincts, your prayers, and your gut—so you can become who you were meant to be? I believe you have it in you.

Yes, it takes practice. It takes intention. You're going to miss the mark, you're going to forget, you're going to mess up. But over time, it will become easier to let the words you choose become a part of you, a part of your story. And when that happens, I believe you're going to see your life more clearly and see yourself more honestly. I believe you're going to be leaning into your potential and your purpose in exciting new ways. I believe you're going to grow and heal, and share that growth and healing with the world. Because you're the only you. And your words, your story—they matter. Your words are powerful, and so are you.

ONE

Believe was one of the very first words I had engraved on keys to give to friends, and there was never any question in my mind that this word would always be in heavy rotation with me. I chose *believe* because there's a great deal of power in the things we choose to believe in, where we place our thoughts and our trust. What we believe in tends to become a lens through which we see the world, the guiding light we use to make decisions and deal with problems, the mirror that reflects how we feel about ourselves. That's no small thing.

Believe is a word that covers quite a bit of ground. Sometimes I choose to focus on beliefs about myself and my abilities. Other times my energy goes to believing in others or in the general goodness of people or in my Higher Power, God. I love all the bases this word covers.

I'd love to tell you that I always focus on high-minded beliefs, but sometimes it can be as simple as getting through a difficult day with my screaming, temperamental children, or trusting that I can take a risk and that it will work, or even choosing to believe that I can change a long-held belief about myself.

Each person's beliefs are as unique as they are. Sometimes those beliefs are based on our personal experiences, both negative and positive, and sometimes we are choosing to embrace or create a new belief (I have to work really hard to deprogram the negative self-talk that comes so naturally).

Being intentional isn't just for goals! When *believe* is your word, it can remind you to be intentional about setting *beliefs* for what you want, what you need, and who you want to become. If your beliefs about yourself and your life are limiting, negative, or even downright toxic, then I guarantee you are living small and you aren't as free and flourished as you could be. To truly live out our potential and purpose, we can't waste time with lies that hold us back. We have to train our minds to believe what we tell them to believe. We can't let our minds control us—it has to be the other way around. We are in control of what we choose to meditate on: things that are life-giving or bleak.

If you've chosen this word, I want to challenge you to stay determined and go after what you want your life to look like. And believe in yourself. You can and will do it.

WRITE IT DOWN

Sometimes just thinking or saying something isn't enough. Writing it down, however, has a way of helping something really sink in. Maybe you don't know exactly what's holding you back. It can be tough to identify all of the ways that all of our negative beliefs affect us, especially at first. After all, most of our thoughts and responses are automatic. We walk into a situation, and after a snap assessment, we default onto a well-traveled belief path that already exists in our brains. It happens so fast that you don't even realize you made a choice based on an existing belief about yourself.

One way to start combatting this habit is to pick up a journal or

You are
exactly what
God had in
mind when
he made you.

—FATHER GREG BOYLE

notebook (or you can use the Notes app on your phone). Start tracking all the little beliefs that pop into your head every day. When you catch yourself falling into a negative spiral, write down what that belief was, cross it out, and then write down a new belief to replace it. For example, if you are feeling anxious in a room full of people you don't know, you might become aware of negative thoughts. So try this activity:

One small, negative belief I have is:

No one cares what I have to say.

_____

_____

**Now cross out the pre-existing negative belief,
and replace it with a new, stronger belief.**

_____

_____

Over time, I promise you will notice a pattern. All of your smaller negative beliefs about yourself will point to something bigger—a unifying belief that connects all those little thoughts and cuts to the core. Maybe your big belief is that you aren't enough. Or that you're too much. Unlovable. Uninteresting. Incapable. Unintelligent. Unworthy. *Ouch!* I'm pretty sure none of us would want our worst enemies to feel that way, but here we are, telling ourselves these horrible things every day. It's time for that to stop. *Now.*

Writing down the lies you believe about yourself will help you become more intentional about noticing them so you can start to change them. Keeping track of the new beliefs you want to embrace will be a huge help. Use these new, rewritten beliefs as affirmations you read to yourself every day or a list you review every so often to remind yourself of how far you've come.

TELL IT LIKE IT IS

Gratitude is one of the biggest ways we can ingrain new, positive beliefs about ourselves and our lives into our brains. This is because expressing gratitude lights up some of the reward pathways in our brains by boosting the production of serotonin and dopamine, two chemicals that are linked to happiness. So it should literally be a no-brainer to incorporate gratitude into our daily routines, right? Except that we're all human and we get distracted, or addicted to the negativity. It's so much easier to focus on what we lack than to be grateful for what we have. Let's break this cycle.

The good news is that you can make being grateful one of your beliefs by getting into the gratitude habit. The easiest way for me to do this has always been through daily affirmations. Choose an affirmation and write it out, or say it to yourself in the mirror. This gives your brain a gratitude workout by forging and strengthening positive pathways, causing the negative pathways to become weak and puny. And seriously, this is a much easier workout than putting in a sweaty hour at the gym!

I want to share some of my personal affirmations with you, and I hope they inspire you to use them or to create special affirmations of your own. Let these affirmations reflect what you want to believe about yourself. Pro tip: pick an affirmation from the notebook you started keeping in the last section!

- I believe I am strong, and I am grateful that I can stand up for myself and others.
- I believe I am capable, and I am grateful for the trust others place in me.
- I believe I am worthy of love, and I am grateful that I have so many people to love in my life.
- I believe I am making a difference in the world, and I am grateful for the difference that has made in me.
- I believe I am beautiful inside and out, and I am grateful for my body that lets me do so many incredible things.
- I believe I am brave, and I am grateful that I can do difficult things.
- I believe I can help others, and I am grateful I have others who can help me.

Let's face it: society, the media, and our own scarred pasts can make it really difficult to embrace good mental health and positive thinking. So what should you do if you have a negative belief so big and all-encompassing that gratitude and daily affirmations like the ones listed here aren't going to even make a dent in that belief? A therapist once told me to think of my brain like a record player. Every time we think a negative thought, it creates a groove. And if we have a negative belief embedded in all parts of our lives, that means the groove is so deep, it'll cause the record to skip and even stall out. With a groove like that, you'll see confirmation and support for your negative belief everywhere you look, and it's really tough to be grateful when all you can see is the worst in yourself.

To change that belief, you need to create a new, deep groove for a positive belief about yourself—an extreme, bold, one-or two-sentence affirmation that's the over-the-top opposite of that negative belief you've been playing on repeat for years. Write it out and put it everywhere. Take the time to focus on the affirmation multiple times throughout the day so you can start singing the new tune. As it sinks in, then it's time to put that statement into action.

Look for what makes you feel excited and full of energy.

If your affirmation is "I believe I am the most capable person in my office," then it's time to start acting like it. How would "the most capable person in your office" start a meeting? How would she volunteer for a new, challenging assignment? How would she attend a networking event? Have you ever heard the phrase "Fake it 'til you make it"? That's exactly what I'm telling you to do. You might feel silly at first, but after a while, your brain will catch up with your actions and affirmations, and you will begin to feel your new belief settle into your soul. You won't just be telling yourself that you are the most capable person—you will *be* the most capable person you can be.

CAST A VISION

If you find yourself struggling with what you want to believe about yourself and your life, I suggest creating a vision board. No glitter glue or puffy paint needed! (Although I welcome any excuse to add glitter into my life.) And no, I'm not talking about a list of things you want to accomplish or earn; I'm talking about creating a vision for how you want to *feel*. Look for things that make you feel like the best, truest version of you, things that make you excited and filled with energy.

Attitude is a choice.
Happiness is a choice.
Optimism is a choice.
Kindness is a choice.
Giving is a choice. Respect
is a choice. Whatever
choice you make makes
you. Choose wisely.

—ROY T. BENNETT

Head to your favorite store (I'm a CVS girl myself!) and pick up poster board, glue, scissors, and a stack of magazines that catch your eye. Choose a time when nothing will distract you, put on your favorite music, and cut out pictures, phrases, or anything else that calls to your soul. There are no limits here, so don't worry that you could never possibly afford to buy a mountain chalet or book first-class tickets for a monthlong jaunt to Italy on your $30,000/year salary. Cut out those pictures anyway! Once you've covered your board, prop it up somewhere and look at it often. Over time, I promise you'll start to see what all of those things have in common. Now you have a jumping-off point to figure out what you really, truly want for yourself, and even which beliefs about yourself are holding you back from living that life you want.

Do you really want to keep missing out on a vision board-worthy life, just because you believe you aren't _____ enough to fight for it or deserve it? Keep *believe* in the forefront of your mind, and challenge those limiting thoughts. Replace them with the belief that you are more than enough to make it happen.

Reflect

I want to leave you with questions to journal about, discuss with a trusted friend, or reflect on. These are the same questions I ask myself when I start a new focus on *believe*. Let these help you get started!

What is something about yourself that you are really unhappy with? What does it make you believe about yourself?

_____

_____

_____

_____

_____

What is the opposite of that belief? How can you write that out as an affirmation to tell yourself daily and begin to act out?

_____

_____

_____

_____

What are you most grateful for in your life?

_____

_____

_____

_____

We named our daughter Love because I firmly believe that there is nothing on earth that is more powerful than love. Love is powerful because of its strength to bind us together, and it is just as powerful because of its vulnerability as it guides us to be more open and honest with one another and with ourselves. The name *Love* felt like the perfect fit for our baby girl, who we hope grows up to be powerful both in strength and in vulnerability and absolutely overflowing with love. Needless to say, this is one of my favorite words.

Love is the most valuable commodity on the planet, and the world is thirsty for more of it. We crave it. We need it. It keeps us alive and nourished. Love is not just a grand feeling of affection that fills you up—although it absolutely is that. It's also a choice and a sacrifice, a noun and a verb. Love is the most valuable gift that you can give, because loving someone consistently day in and day out is a decision that you make. It's an action. Love can be small, intimate acts as well as big, sweeping gestures. It requires patience when you feel anything but calm, kindness when you would rather be cutting, giving grace and forgiveness when you could easily stay angry and resentful. Choosing love makes your life fuller, richer, and deeper, even on the worst days.

When you choose *love* as your word to focus on, you are making a commitment to loving others and yourself, both in feeling and in action. Imagine if we could actually see love as we walked through the world each day—a warm pink glow surrounding everyone and everything, brighter and bigger around those who love themselves and others with abandon, and smaller and duller around others who hoard their love, afraid they will be hurt if they give it away.

When this is your word, you are choosing to see the world through love-colored glasses, to

> **All you need is love. Love is all you need.**
>
> —JOHN LENNON AND PAUL MCCARTNEY

EVERY WORD MATTERS

grow your own aura of love as big and bright as it can be, and to share it without question with those with the smallest glow. Are you ready?

LET LOVE IN

Love can feel like a dangerous word to some people. If you've never felt loved or have too often felt the pain of losing love, you may have closed your heart to it. You don't want to feel the sting of heartbreak, so you don't let love in. You like people well enough; you enjoy spending time with them, but you aren't willing to be vulnerable and take a chance on loving people and letting them love you in return. That's a really lonely way to go through life. If you are feeling this way, then *love* is a great word for you to choose.

We all *need* love. We need it as much as air or water or food. There is no way to live a full, powerful, wild, wonderful life without love. We can't put down roots, grow, and blossom without the nourishment that love provides. A life without love is stunted, small, and so much less than it should be. I don't want that for you! I want us all to be living big lives brimming with love. Don't you?

START WITH YOU

The love that so many of us lack is a love for ourselves. When we look in the mirror, we often see only our flaws, our scars, and all the ways we aren't enough instead of seeing all the ways we are beautiful, strong, inspiring, capable, and magical.

Close your eyes and think about yourself. Think about what you're good at, your dreams, your habits, your thoughts. How do you feel about yourself? Warm and fuzzy? Lukewarm? Cold and ashamed? Do the same with your story. Think about your journey, your choices, where you are now, and where you want to be. How do you feel about the story you're telling yourself? Now think about the people in your life. How do you feel about your friends, family, romantic partner, colleagues, and people in general? If you are feeling anything less than warm, fuzzy, and empathetic about any of these things, it's definitely time to inject more love for yourself into your life.

I want you to write down everything about yourself, your story, and your relationships that leaves you feeling cold when you think about

them. Why do you think each of those things feels so devoid of love? Is it because of fear? Shame? Pain? Whatever the reason, this is the time for you to explore those thoughts and how they impact your story.

I struggled for years to really love myself because of shame I carried around about my body. Years of working in entertainment, where every casting agent, director, agent, and producer feels free to make comments about all the ways you could be sexier and more appealing, coupled with feeling different because my body didn't look how I thought it should (aka like everyone else's!), left me with very little love for myself. I finally hit a point when I was exhausted from carrying that much shame, disgust, and pain around with me. I wanted to love myself, but I didn't know how.

I started with being intentional. When I had the idea for *Love Your Flawz*, it was because I desperately needed to address my insecurities and find a way to love them. I took the time to figure out where the pain and shame were coming from, and then I began the difficult work of forgiving myself for the choices I'd made, the feelings I'd had, and all the ways I'd let myself down because of it. I also made a choice to forgive all of the people whose opinions and comments had painfully contributed to my feelings (sometimes it's not a feeling, it's a choice . . . but the feelings tend to follow), and I forgave myself for believing them. I replaced those toxic beliefs with new, lovely, custom-made ones I wrote myself. I came out the other side so much lighter. All of those loveless feelings had been taking up too much space. As I let them go, floating away like a feather, I found so much room left for that potent, tangible love for myself and for others.

DON'T HOLD BACK

I want you to do the same thing. Identify what has been holding you back from loving yourself, and then begin to inspect it, question it, and forgive it. I'm not suggesting you call up the ex who made you believe horrible things about yourself and tell him you forgive him. No, this forgiveness is for *you*. This is looking at a belief you were given by someone else, deciding it no longer belongs in your story, replacing it with a new belief motivated by love, and then letting the old one go like dust in the wind. Self-love, at its core, is holding that tension between knowing you

We know what the world wants from us. We know we must decide whether to stay small, quiet, and uncomplicated or allow ourselves to grow as big, loud, and complex as we were made to be. Every girl must decide whether to be true to herself or true to the world. Every girl must decide whether to settle for adoration or fight for love.

—GLENNON DOYLE

were created with unique imperfections, and also coming to accept that you are in charge of your story, that you can write it to be anything you want, and then choosing to write something beautiful. It's embracing *you* as you are, while forgiving the past and leaving room for you to grow and change in the future.

You may be able to do this on your own, or you may need help—I know I did! Talking with a therapist or counselor can be so beneficial as you do this work. Helping others achieve self-love and good mental health is a therapist's life work, her passion and purpose. Don't hold back from seeking that help. There are no awards in life for healing your wounds all by yourself.

LOVE IN ACTION

Learning to love ourselves and give ourselves grace will allow us to love others in their perfectly imperfect humanity. Even if your social circle is small, your impact on others in the world doesn't have to be. Think of everyone you interact with every day, from your partner to your coworkers to the barista at your favorite coffee shop to the produce manager at the grocery store. It can be all too easy to float through life and forget how our interactions can make or ruin someone else's day. We're all awfully fragile, if you think about it.

We all need one another, and our actions and words affect one another deeply. We all need to be reminded of grace, to forgive ourselves and others. It's the only way we can have loving, healthy relationships. Let's all soften our hearts toward one another, and try to remember that everyone is fighting their own battles. When you treat others with love and empathy, they notice and feel that energy and impact. Some people are even starved for it. Your love helps nourish their souls so they can nourish others in turn. Think how many loving chain reactions you could start by freely pouring out love to everyone you come into contact with!

Loving and serving go hand in hand, because serving others is really the physical manifestation of the feeling. It's love in action. Whether you are serving your family, your friends, or your community, you are demonstrating love each time you do something for someone else without expecting anything in return. And—bonus!—when you

WAYS TO BOOST SELF-LOVE

— Make *you* a priority and do things that nurture you, make you stronger, and make you proud of who you are and how you live your life. If you don't feel the love for yourself yet, start acting like you do.

— Serve others with a generous heart. Serving others who are either strong or struggling will help you find a new perspective on your feelings about yourself.

— See a therapist or a counselor. Talking through your issues can help you get to the root of why you struggle to love yourself. Tip: Don't get stuck on the *why*. You can take time to explore and to understand, but then fight through those issues to move on and get to the solutions and resolutions.

— Remind yourself that you are not alone in your feelings.

There is a reason so many books and songs have been written about this topic. Everyone struggles with love!

— When people pay you a compliment or say they love you, don't look for reasons why they weren't sincere. Let their words sink in and believe them.

— Ask your people why they love you. Jot down their answers, and carry them with you. When you are feeling unlovable, pull them out to remind yourself of why you *are* lovable!

serve others, the love in your own heart grows and multiplies. (That is, if your motives are clean and you're not over-giving out of an empty tank.) When it comes from a pure heart, for the sake of love itself and not for an ulterior motive, seeing how our service helps others can give us a love high. That's why it's important to fill up our tanks with self-care and self-love first, because as they say, you need to put on your oxygen mask first before you can put on anyone else's. Experiment with this one. Whether you've mastered self-love or not, you can be tired and grouchy when you walk through the door, but choosing to serve someone else will oftentimes help some of your dreary feelings drop away, and love will rush in to take their place.

Just as a reminder, serving others doesn't have to be onerous or difficult. Here are a few ideas for ways you can serve:

- Start with something you already love doing. Ask yourself how you can use that thing to serve someone else.
- If you love cooking, take yourself down to the local soup kitchen and get to work!
- If you love reading, volunteer to read at your local nursing home.
- If you love knitting, why not

> **There is no straight line to Goodness, to Love, or to God. And thank God, Grace is always retroactive.**
>
> —RICHARD ROHR

knit scarves and donate them to an organization that could use them?

- If you love shopping, why not offer to go grocery shopping for your elderly neighbor or for a friend who just had a baby?

There is no act of service too small. If you serve even one person, you are making a rosy pink mark for love. Over time, those little love marks add up to paint a more beautiful, loving world. Let's all keep working until those love-colored glasses show the truth—a world where everyone is wrapped up safely in love!

Reflect

I want to leave you with questions to journal about, discuss with a trusted friend, or reflect on. These are the same questions I ask myself when I am thirsty for love.

What does the word **love** mean to you?

_____

_____

_____

When do you feel the most loved? Why?

_____

_____

How can you make someone else
feel loved in the same way?

_____

_____

_____

_____

_____

In what ways can you open up more love in your life?

_____

_____

_____

_____

THREE

Who we'll be tomorrow is not defined by who we were yesterday. Each of us has the potential to grow and change all of the time. What takes us from where we are now to where we want to be are our dreams—for ourselves, for what we want, and for our dreams for the world around us.

Our ability to dream is what keeps us alive and growing, thriving and striving. Without dreaming, we'd all stay in the same place, just reacting to what life throws at us. Instead, we dream, and those dreams lead to plans, which lead to steps, which lead to action, which lead to change. When you choose *dream* as your word, you are choosing to cast a vision for your future. You are choosing to take a serious, honest dive into your heart, and then paint a picture for yourself of what you *really* want your life to look like. And if the life you've been living doesn't look like the life you've been dreaming, you are choosing to do the work to chase those dreams until reality and your dreams align.

I'm sure you already have a number of dreams that you've been nurturing. Maybe you've always dreamed of becoming a mother, or writing a novel, or traveling to Italy, or landing *the* job. Or maybe your dream is to help endangered animals or, like me, to find creative ways to support people transitioning out of homelessness. I love that Martin Luther King Jr.'s dream in his famous "I Have a Dream" speech wasn't just about him. This dream was about an injustice he wanted to fight, a way he wanted to change the world for the better. Yes, of course, we can and should have dreams for ourselves, but I believe the best dreams *also* include other people's healing and well-being.

So often the dreams that end up sticking are the ones that combine passion with purpose, what we want for ourselves with what we want to do to help others. Those are the dreams that gain momentum and take on a life of their own that is so much bigger and more incredible than anything we could dream up on our own. So, as you focus on *dream*, don't hold yourself back.

EVERY WORD MATTERS

I have a dream that my four little children will one day live in a nation where they will not be judged by the color of their skin, but by the content of their character.

—MARTIN LUTHER KING JR.

NO DREAM TOO BIG

The biggest pushback I hear on *dream* is when people say their dreams aren't practical, that the odds of achieving them are too small to risk anything to get them. But I say there is no dream too big. Is there a dream you have, but it feels so far-fetched that it's not worth pursuing? Maybe there is a passion you've had since you were little. Maybe it's a new desire you just can't seem to fully ignore. I know you have a dream in you. It may seem like the world is telling you that you can't make it happen, or that it doesn't make sense, or that it's not worth it, or that it's too extreme, too difficult. But we know the truth, right? You *can* do this. Whatever it is your soul is whispering to you, I want you to run after it with all your strength.

Some dreams will end up looking different than what you expected. You'll hit a dead end or a closed door. Listen to your intuition or your inner Peace-O-Meter, as I like to call it, to know when you need to knock down that closed door to fight for it and also when it's time to let that old version of your dream go.

But if you have to let it go, that doesn't mean your dream is dead. It just may need to be dusted off, reimagined, and repurposed. Like an embossed key necklace that's been passed from person to person, you can trust that your dream is going to take you to exactly where you're meant to go. If you find yourself staring at a dream dead end, look around. Is there a smaller, more overgrown path that didn't seem like the way to your dream at the time? Try it. Often what seems like a detour turns out to be the exact path you needed. It may be the road that reshapes your dream and reveals your true purpose—the one that only you can fulfill. Every road we take helps turn us into who we were always meant to become.

So don't limit yourself before you even start. Go for the big dreams (and the small ones too), and hold those dreams loosely so you can notice when they pull you in a new direction, or morph and grow into dreams you never knew you wanted. Your final destination may not be exactly what you dreamed at the very beginning—it may be even better!

DREAM LIKE YOU MEAN IT

My guess is that you've chosen *dream* as your word because you are ready and excited to make some changes in your life. Maybe you are just graduating from college and ready to take on the world. Or maybe you've been killing time in a *meh* job to save money to launch your own business. Whatever your situation, the first step in making big changes is to figure out where you're going. And to do that, you have to make dreaming a priority.

My recommendation is to start by taking a day, a weekend, or even just an afternoon and making it your dream time. Go somewhere that inspires you, but make sure it's somewhere you won't be interrupted—like your favorite coffee shop, a park, or your own backyard. My favorite spot to dream is nestled in my hammock swing in my front yard, or sitting at a favorite restaurant and people-watching, observing what they seem to want and need below the surface. Bring a notebook and a pen, and write anything, big or small, related to what you want your life to look like, such as:

- What makes your heart come alive?
- What injustice do you see in your community that you'd like to change?
- What dreams do you already have?
- What activities and hobbies do you love?

- What do you think you want to do with your life?
- What fills you with joy?
- What breaks your heart, and how would you like to change this?
- What skills and gifts do you have that you want to use?
- Where would you want to live?
- Where do you want to visit?
- What makes you feel alive?

Over the next few days or weeks, reread these lists. You'll begin to see patterns. Write the patterns you see on a blank page.

- Do those patterns remind you of anything?
- Do they connect to a certain type of job? A certain lifestyle?
- Do they spark anything specific in your heart or whisper anything deep down?

Take time each day to think about these lists and patterns. Meditate about them. Pray over them. Be patient and listen. Let it all coalesce into a vision for your life that is so *you* that you just can't wait to pursue it.

Already have a dream you want to chase? Great! Write out every-thing related to that dream: action steps, feelings, locations, vibe, budget. Pray and meditate over all of that, and listen for the nudge inside that will show you where to start, or watch as your dream gains clarity and structure in your mind.

MAKE IT BIGGER

If your dream is just about your passions, it's perhaps smaller than it could be. I want to challenge you to think through how your dream could include making a difference in the world. We all have a purpose—something that we are uniquely equipped to do to make an impact. When passion meets purpose, we all win.

I think my dreams have always included my purpose in some form or another—and I bet yours do too, if you look a little more closely. When I was pursuing an acting career, I joined forces with Brie Larson to launch the *Love Your Flawz* movement to encourage women to embrace their so-called flaws as the things that make them special. It was a message I desperately needed to hear too. When I shifted my focus to my songwriting and singing, I toured the country performing, spreading inspiration, and connecting with fans at shows—that's where The Giving Keys was born!

Since The Giving Keys became my full-time gig, I've worked to encourage and inspire women with our pay-it-forward-message jewelry and to help people transition out of homelessness. No matter which of my dreams I was chasing, my purpose has never changed. It's always been to encourage women to love themselves exactly as they are and celebrate the imperfections that make them special instead of covering them up.

I'm so thankful that our purpose and our jobs aren't always the same thing. I've tried to use every job I've had as a platform to expand my purpose. (I even sold homemade, bedazzled belts and rhinestone "Jesus is my homeboy" T-shirts from behind the counter when I was a coffee barista!) And if my job running The Giving Keys ended tomorrow, you'd still be able to find me shouting out my purpose on my podcast, clothing line, interviews, and eventually as part of whatever dream I come up with next. My purpose is woven into all of my dreams, making those dreams bigger, more impactful, and more urgent than if they were focused only on what I wanted for myself.

DREAM TOGETHER

You don't have to dream alone, you know. Find other dreamers! Pursuing a dream can sometimes feel lonely, especially when passion takes over and you find yourself working as fast as you can to make it happen. I think a lot of us have a tendency not to share our dreams with the people in our lives until we are already succeeding because we don't want to be embarrassed if we fail. But if we don't share our dreams, we miss out on the encouragement our friends and family give to help keep us going. We miss out on the connections they can help us make or the opportunities they may have for us. And we miss out on the joy of celebrating the little wins with the people who see and appreciate how hard we're working to make those dreams happen.

Even if you already have supportive friends and family, it's worthwhile to seek out and surround yourself with other women who are

dreaming as big as you are. These may be the friends you already have, but they may not be. These dreamers may be other women who also want to start nonprofits whom you can compare loan terms and tax burdens with, or fellow actors you can run lines with and commiserate with after auditions, or they may be #girlboss mentors who can chat with you about content calendars, engagement, and brand deals in a way your close friends can't.

Meet for a hike, brunch, a beach stroll, or happy hour once a month and check in with each another. Offer suggestions and share resources. Remember, a rising tide lifts all ships. When one of you succeeds, celebrate big, because you never know what opportunities may open up for all of you as a result. Motivate and encourage one another, especially when your dreams feel stalled or you hit setbacks. Look for ways your dreams and their dreams could potentially combine, taking both dreams to new heights and giving you an interesting partner to work with.

There's no wrong way to dream. I just hope that as long as *dream* is your word, you let your dreams run wild and grow bigger, better, and stronger until they are worthy of you and the impact you were born to make on this generation and world.

Reflect

I want to leave you with questions to journal about, discuss with a trusted friend, or reflect on. These are the same questions I ask myself when I start to dream.

What makes you come alive with passion?

_____

_____

_____

_____

_____

_____

What ideas keep popping in your head over and over and create a bubbling energy inside your mind and heart?

_____

_____

_____

_____

What inspires you to live a life full of love
for your neighbors and yourself?

_____

_____

_____

_____

faith

You may be wondering why I included both *believe* and *faith* as key words—I mean, those words mean pretty much the same thing, right? Well, not exactly. There is definitely a difference; let me explain.

Faith has always been a challenging word for me. I was a philosophy major, not to mention a classic overthinker who likes to do my research right down to the details. I want proof. I want to be able to see and touch and hear and feel what I believe in. And that works fine for many parts in life.

For example, in my own life, I absolutely research someone before I believe in them enough to hire them to help run my company. I get inspections and look at the maintenance history of a house before I believe it's safe enough for my family to live in. Makes sense, right? But there are some things I'll never be able to adequately research, or see and touch and feel before I can believe in them. For those things, all I have to follow are little breadcrumbs of information, never seeing or knowing the big picture. Those things require faith.

For me, faith means going from crumb to crumb, letting them show you there is something or someone bigger than you out there. A light to guide you when everything around you is shrouded in darkness. An otherworldly feeling of love and care that you can't prove, but that you certainly can't ignore. A Higher Power.

And we know that in all things God works for the good.

—ROMANS 8:28

Faith is much deeper than mere belief. It's the bone-deep soul knowledge that there is something—some*one*—far greater who will guide you to your best path, guide you to your greatest purpose, and love you no matter what. When I focus on faith, I want to draw closer to God and to remind myself that it's okay if I feel out of control because I know that He's got me.

WHEN FAITH FALTERS

I know I'm not alone in struggling with my faith sometimes. Faith can be so challenging because it requires almost blind trust in what we cannot see, touch, taste, feel, or hear. Our senses provide safe, concrete evidence and certainty. It's easy to have faith when life is going well, but it can become so much more difficult when we're experiencing trouble or profoundly devastating circumstances.

I'm certainly no exception. There have been plenty of times when my faith has been tested by situations that took almost everything I had out of me. One time, the church I'd attended and loved for years went through dark betrayals and stopped being a safe space. After a scandal involving our youth leader rocked the congregation, our lead pastor lost his struggle with cancer and passed away. The new leadership brought about chaos and unhealthy, twisted, scary theology. Once I left, I felt completely lost. I had always felt that God was watching over me, but instead I felt confused.

I tried going to different churches, craving that connection and

sense of fulfillment and belonging, but I couldn't bring myself to trust an "institution" again. However, I just couldn't let it all go completely. I started a Philosophy Night with friends once a week. We'd ask and debate the questions that none of us could answer, poring over philosophy books and trying to find anything that had a ring of truth.

There was a turning point when I visited with Franciscan friars at a monastery in the Bronx. I was in awe of how deeply they embraced God's teachings, spending their entire lives serving, helping, and encouraging the poor. The friars had a humble, servant-hearted, peaceful reverence for God I had never seen before. It couldn't have been further from the modern church I'd grown up in, with its smoke machines and rock concert worship. Spending time with the friars renewed my hope.

I realized I hadn't actually been searching for a new church; I'd been searching for some proof that God was real after having my faith beaten and bruised. What I learned along the way was that I had to be okay with not having all the answers. I had to learn to live in the tension of uncertainty and the unknown. Life can be full of breathtaking beauty and love and deep kindness, but it can also have sharp edges and difficult situations and impossible choices. None of us are ever guaranteed a firm place to stand. That's where faith comes in. Even in my greatest moments of doubting, I can't freely live without a connection to and reliance on God. And that is real enough for me.

If your faith has faltered, I would encourage you to do your own searching and research. Look into the history and origins of your faith's traditions and customs. Which teachings are specific to your community, and which are intrinsic to your faith? Look around at your faith community and take stock. We can all benefit from learning from others who share our faith, but if the people you have surrounded yourself with aren't reflecting what you know your faith is really about, it may be time to find a new community. Look for people who have a faith that challenges and bolsters yours. Seek out people who allow you to ask questions and have doubts. Surround yourself with people whose authenticity, love, and passion set your faith on fire. Those are your people. Hold onto them.

> **Faith consists in believing when it is beyond the power of reason to believe.**
>
> —VOLTAIRE

FAITH OUT LOUD

One of the simplest ways to deepen your faith is to simply talk to God and trust Him to answer in a way that only a Higher Power can. There are many ways to do this. You can pray formally, on your knees, journal your thoughts, talk out loud while you lie in bed, or contemplate while you fold laundry or drive your car. There really is no wrong way to reach out, and nothing is off-limits.

There is nothing you can say to God that He hasn't heard before. Sometimes just admitting your worries, problems, issues, and anxieties can give you a measure of peace—and that release can lead to a feeling of relief and serenity. But a huge part of faith is truly believing that God can answer those prayers.

Try writing out your prayers (or at least jot down what you prayed for). Keep a prayer tracker, a journal, or even a box filled with your prayers scribbled on paper. This can be a great tool to help you see your faith more clearly. After some time has passed, go back and review what you've written down. How have your prayers been answered? How many were answered in ways you never expected? How many were answered in a way that was better than you could have imagined? Over time you will see all of the wonderful ways God is working in your life.

BREATHE DEEP

I have a breathing exercise I do whenever I'm feeling overwhelmed by a problem and I don't have a solution. This exercise helps me lean into my faith instead of assuming that I have to solve everything all by myself. We all need to be reminded that many things are out of our control.

FAITH IN YOURSELF

As women, we have often been conditioned not to make a fuss, not to be too loud, and not to stand out too much. We've also been encouraged to let others make decisions for us. To find faith in ourselves, we have to start listening to our instincts and trusting our choices. You can call

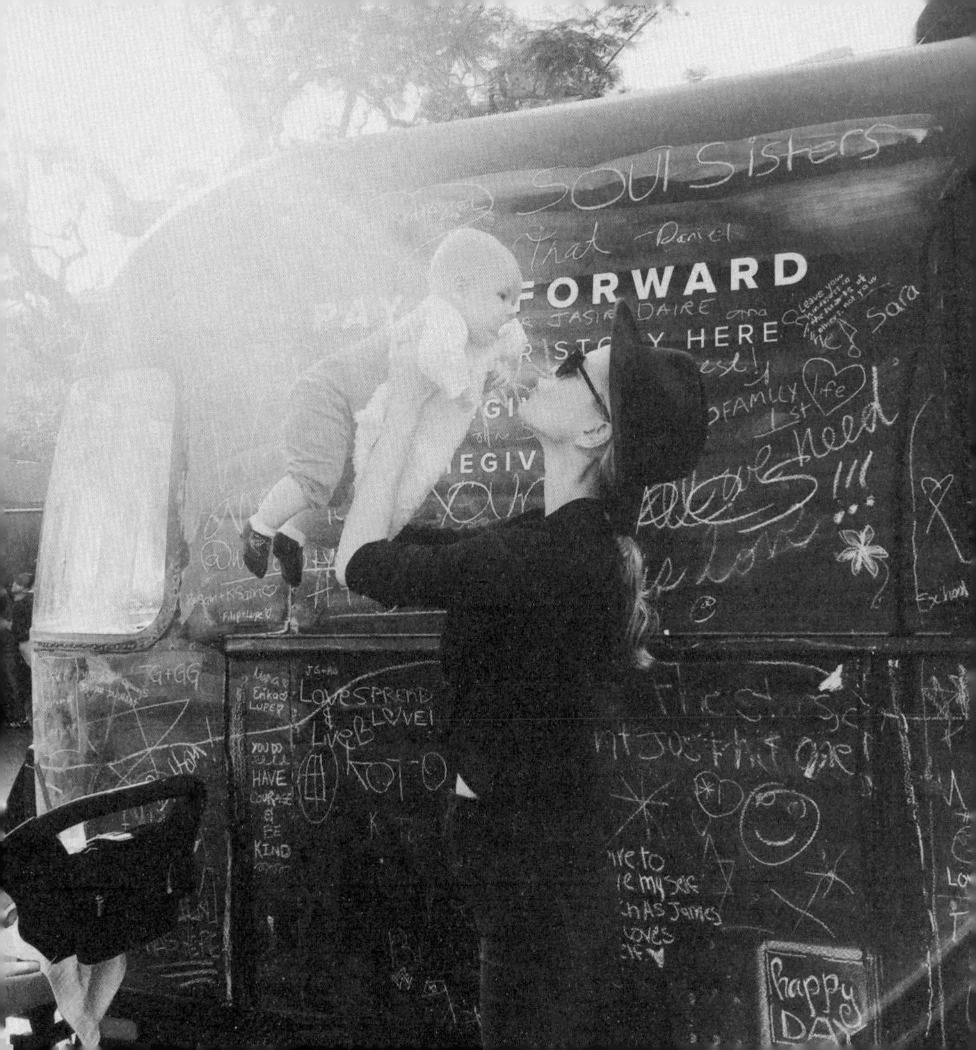

SOUl Sisters
FORWARD
happy

To start, find somewhere quiet where you have some privacy. You can shut the door to your office or bedroom, sit alone in your car, or even duck into the restroom. Sit and close your eyes, and then follow these steps:

- Inhale deeply for a count of three. As you breathe in, focus on what is upsetting you, and picture it clearly in your mind.
- After inhaling, hold your breath for a count of three. While you do this, tell yourself that God will provide a solution for the stressful situation or thought. You don't have to think of a specific solution or even steps to find a solution—just focus on the fact that the right solution will be found.
- Then exhale for a count of three. While you release your breath, mentally release the issue you are struggling with. Let it go.
- Repeat as many times as you need until you start to feel at peace that a solution is coming.

it your intuition, gut, instinct—or even my personal choice, your Peace-O-Meter. But whatever you call it, it's time to start listening to the little voice that nudges you when a situation is a little off, or urges you to take a running leap and go for something despite the odds.

As you focus on faith, I want you to extend that faith to yourself and to your Peace-O-Meter. Because no matter how messy you might feel like your life is, I promise that *you* are also worth having faith in. There will never be another person exactly like you in this world, another woman who has experienced what you have, has the friends and family you have, has been to every place you have, and has impacted the lives you have. You are here for a purpose, to make an impact on this world. Even if it doesn't feel like it right now, you *will* make waves. Isn't that worth having faith in? While *faith* is your word, I want to challenge you to listen for your Peace-O-Meter, even if it's only a whisper, and use it as your guide. Don't second-guess yourself or ignore it. See how far you can go when you have faith in *you*.

Reflect

I want to leave you with questions to journal about, discuss
with a trusted friend, or reflect on. These are the same questions I ask myself when I aim to deepen my faith.

Who and what do you have faith in? Write it out in detail.

_____

_____

_____

_____

_____

_____

_____

What aspects of your faith do you have questions or doubts about? Write out those questions. Make a list of people and resources that may be able to help you tackle those questions.

_____

_____

_____

Do you feel that you have faith in yourself? If not, what exactly is holding you back? How can you grow greater faith in yourself?

_____

_____

_____

_____

_____

fearl

Fearless is one of those words that gives me the shivers (in a good way). It feels strong and daring and a little bit rebellious. Being fearless, at least to me, means living life to the fullest every day and going after what you want with an almost reckless abandon. It's taking big risks, fighting important fights, and jumping right into the deep end without hesitation. It's swimming through life's deepest oceans to discover all the magical things waiting on the other shore.

Of course, living fearless doesn't guarantee success. There is always risk when you choose to leap into the great unknown. Part of being fearless is acknowledging that you *could* fail, but not letting that hold you back from taking the risk—because you could also succeed!

Being fearless is about sacrificing the safe and comfortable to gain something new and precious. Being fearless is knowing what you want, owning it, and yelling it out to the world, all while Making. It. Happen. When you choose *fearless* as the word to focus on and infuse into your life, you are ready to start something extraordinarily breathtaking without letting fear slow you down or hold you back.

NO REGRETS

I think a huge part of letting *fearless* into your life is looking at all you've already done and taking stock. Where have you been fearless about pursuing what you want up to this point? Are there things that you regret not doing? As much as we try to accept our pasts with grace, I think we all have a few things we've done that we may regret, but we all have way *more* things we regret that we *haven't* done. We may regret the person we walked by without speaking to, the promotion we didn't ask for, the pay raise we didn't negotiate, or the risk we didn't go for because it felt too uncomfortable, too risky. Today is the day you say, "No more." No more regrets. No more playing it safe. No more choosing the path of least resistance, especially when it doesn't even take you where you want to go.

Now think through all of the different moments you want to experience in this life, both now and in the future. Write them all down. Think about moments you desire internally, externally, emotionally, goal-and-career-wise, adventure-wise, tangible and intangible, etc. I bet it's a long list, huh? That's okay. There is no such thing as wanting too much for your one wild, wonderful life. It's also beautiful and complete to desire nothing more than what you already have, to learn to be present and grateful for simplicity. Maybe it's more fearless for you to let go of wanting more. Only you know deep down what your soul needs.

Look at your list. Let yourself want all of those things. I bet there are a few that really jump out at you—the ones you want more than anything else. The desires that matter in a way that some of the other ones on your list don't. You

> **Be fearless in the pursuit of what sets your soul on fire.**
>
> —JENNIFER LEE

don't want to regret never going after *those* things. So let's get fearless about those things. Let's write down all the circumstances, challenges, and obstacles standing in our way, and then let's start peacefully, yet intentionally, brainstorming how to overcome them.

To be honest, you will absolutely fail. There isn't a successful person out there who hasn't failed spectacularly many times. Being fearless means being okay with failure. In fact, it means *embracing* failure. When *fearless* is your word, you'll be taking chances and dancing with risk, knowing full well that you will stumble, take breaks, and even fall flat on your face. But you will welcome each setback and failure, knowing that you learn a great deal more when you stumble than you do when you succeed.

Every failure opens up your eyes to ways to make your heart better, stronger, and more likely to succeed in the end. It would be marvelous if there were a foolproof manual that showed you how to make any and every dream come true. But since that manual doesn't exist, the only way to learn is to try different things and see what works. Allow yourself a little time and grace to feel frustrated, sad, or embarrassed when everything falls apart. Let yourself feel and sit in the grief. Then dust

yourself off, figure out what you've learned, and start again with more knowledge than you had before.

ANYTHING, NOT EVERYTHING

Here's another other thing most people don't think about. When you go all in on something that's deeply important to you, then you don't have as much time for the other things in your life. And that is 100 percent okay. You can do anything—I truly believe that—but you can't do *everything*. Or, at least, not all at once. And I am giving you permission right now not to feel guilty about it.

As women, we have somehow come to believe that we must do it *all*—and at the same time. That we can be a prepared #boss at work, an attentive wife and mother at home, a gourmet chef, a flawless interior decorator, a Zen yogi, and a self-care queen, all while keeping our homes sparkling clean. But *no one* can do all of that at once.

If you are spending every spare minute getting your business off the ground to give it the attention it needs, it's almost impossible to get a home-cooked meal on the table every night and the laundry folded and the floors mopped. If you are bulking up your résumé to land your dream job or sending in all the paperwork and applications to your chosen university, then you may not have time to be as adventurous or as social as you'd like. If you have a newborn baby you are struggling to feed, care for, and get on a sleep schedule, well, you won't be able to put in those extra hours at work for a while.

You aren't inadequate because you aren't Wonder Woman. Unless you legitimately have superpowers that I don't know about, you can't be all things to all people all the time. At some point, you have to choose.

LET IT GO

Let's all take a page out of Queen Elsa's book (anyone else seen *Frozen* five hundred times with their kids?) and let some things go. You were made to make an impact on the world like only *you* can. To take that spark within and light a flame for good that spreads into your community. To live out your one-of-a-kind purpose. Those are some pretty big

The cave you fear to enter holds the treasure you seek.

—JOSEPH CAMPBELL

asks. When you are busy doing big things, a lot of your time and energy is required.

So I want to challenge you to try out my "should do" swaps from this list for the next month, and spend the time you save on something you want to do—guilt free! Own your choices, and don't apologize for even a second about making time for what matters most.

PRIORITIZE

It's not a failure to be a human with limits. Accept that you alone can't do all the things all the time, and then do your best to banish the guilt. To help ease yourself into this, I want you to start "failing" intentionally. Look at your list of responsibilities, and choose which things to let go of or fail at. Make it a conscious choice to say, "I'm not going to worry about that today," and then, you know, don't.

I have a neighbor who taught me the beauty of letting things go with intention and without shame. She was a mother with a high-powered job, and instead of trying to cram her day full of different obligations

"SHOULD DO" SWAPS

- Skip the early morning gym session for some extra snuggle time with your husband, kids, dog, or yourself (everyone needs to sometimes give themselves some much-needed self-compassion hugs).
- Pick up takeout instead of cooking a meal for a night (or all week—no judgment here!).
- Rock that top knot instead of styling your hair.
- Swap happy hour for a hot Epsom salt bath and an early bedtime.
- Instead of volunteering for anything extra (work project, PTA, room mom), use that time to invest in your pet project.
- Buy a cake instead of baking something for a coworker's birthday. Or better yet, let someone else step up to handle it.
- Use dry shampoo instead of washing your hair every day.

- Just say no to taking an extra shift when you don't want to—no need to explain your reasons.
- Watch the movie or find a summary online instead of reading the book for book club.
- Duck out of work on time instead of offering to plan the office party.
- Resist making a Pinterest-worthy snack for your kid's playdate—Goldfish crackers are fine!
- Do a quick tidy-up (smash/pile/shove things into your closet) instead of cleaning your house before company comes over. Your guests won't notice your dusty baseboards, I promise!
- Take a break from posting on social media—which includes scrolling through just to like your friends' posts. They'll forgive you. Use that time to play with your kids or call your bestie to actually catch up.
- Go for a run to help de-stress instead of putting in more time at work.

- Budget for and hire a cleaning service to handle spring cleaning, and take your kids to the beach or on a peaceful hike.
- Drop your laundry off to be washed, folded, and pressed instead of spending all weekend doing it yourself. Use that time for whatever you want!

and feeling guilty when she inevitably failed to do a mile-long list of things, she accepted her own limits. She told me, "There are only so many hours in a day, and I have to decide how I want to use them." She wasn't wasting time beating herself up for not visiting her parents more, or not seeing her friends for happy hour, or not volunteering for the PTA. She fully owned where she was in life. Her choices gave her the fearlessness she needed to pursue what was most important to her with intention and focus. Her choices gave her the kind of freedom I wanted for myself.

So I came up with my own mantra: Every day, let yourself fail at something. I decided to let go of any fears about failing because failing intentionally was a reminder to myself that failure is inevitable. As I put this into practice, I found that my biggest priorities are taking care of my kids, being intentional about connecting with my husband, being a caring boss and business owner for my employees, and taking time to be present for myself. As much as I love my friends, I became okay with "failing as a friend" and skipping "important" networking events and dinners to be able to spend quality time with my family after a long day at the office. I found I was okay with failing at certain things if it meant I had time to get my mind settled with yoga and have breakfast with my kiddos, even if I couldn't go the extra mile on a work project, fully shower, and get "all done up" for work meetings (dry shampoo for the win!). After a few months of this practice, these choices didn't actually feel like "failures" anymore. They felt like healthy boundaries and healthy decisions.

BE PRESENT

Another big part of challenging yourself to be fearless is living in the moment. It can be so easy to get sucked into anxious thoughts about all the things you need to do, all the places you need to go, or everything that could go wrong. But when you let that happen, you miss out on enjoying the gifts of the here and now. All of that anxiety and worry is just fear dressed up in a fancier outfit. When you are fearless, you embrace learning from all the ways life goes wrong, so why give in to fear in your own thoughts?

Be mindful of your thoughts, and when you feel anxious ones creeping in, redouble your efforts to give 100 percent of yourself to all of the steps that will take you where you want to be. If you focus on being present right where you are, you will find yourself more serene, more creative, and more open to taking advantage of opportunities that cross your path. You'll become more resistant to living small and staying comfortable or trapped when you could break out of your comfort zone to live a colorful life, relishing all its flavors.

Reflect

I want to leave you with questions to journal about, discuss with a trusted friend, or reflect on. These are the same questions I ask myself when I need to be fearless.

What do you most regret not doing? Why didn't you do it?

_____

What is holding you back from going all in on it now?

_____

Which of your responsibilities could you let go of or outsource to give yourself more time for your top priorities?

_____

What is **the** thing you couldn't forgive yourself for if you didn't accomplish or fight for it? Why is this so important to you?

_____

_____

What is holding you back from going all in on it now? What steps can you take to ensure you keep moving forward?

_____

_____

How will you fearlessly pursue that thing?

_____

_____

_____

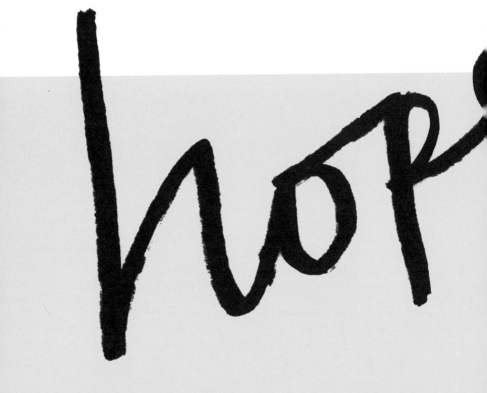

SIX

Hope is hands down my favorite word. I can live without a lot of things, but hope is definitely not one of them. In fact, if I were forced to choose one word as my word forever, it would be *hope*.

Hope is that little flicker of light that guides you through the dark when you feel all is lost and there are no options left. It's the tiny voice that whispers, "You can make it," even when you aren't sure you can. Hope keeps us moving forward, even when we are completely broken. That soft, persistent spark of hope is enough to light a fire of renewal and healing out of the ashes of our darkest moments and most difficult seasons.

As long as you have hope, you have something to work toward, something to cling to even when it feels like you'll be swept away by the storm you're going through. If we lose hope, we really *are* lost. See why I can't live without it?

Hope is the thing with feathers—that perches in the soul—and sings the tune without the words—and never stops—at all.

At its core, hope is a belief or trust that something you desire will happen. Of course, that doesn't always mean it will be in the package you expected or look like you think it will. When *hope* is your word, you focus on opening your eyes to find meaning and opportunities all around you, along with all the ways your life has been made richer by the things you've hoped for and the things you have hope in.

If you find yourself struggling through difficult circumstances or a challenging season, *hope* is the perfect word for you. When you choose hope, you are telling yourself that all is not lost and that better times and better experiences are waiting in your future. There is, and always will be, a light at the end of the tunnel. It's a powerful word to choose to focus on, and *hope* can provide a lot of comfort when you need it most.

BIGGER

If you are going through something painful or difficult, you may be looking for someone or something to give you the hope you can't seem to find. Maybe you need to have hope in the doctors and nurses treating a family member. Maybe you need to have hope in your friends and family who are trying to help you. Maybe you need to have hope in yourself that you can do difficult things. Maybe you need to have hope in God. Luckily, you can have hope in as many things as you need.

You might be surprised where your hope comes from—a beautiful sunny day during a rainy week, a kind word from a stranger, a spontaneous heartfelt hug from your son, a call from an old friend, a glorious sunset that paints the sky pink and gold, or even just a perfect cup of coffee. Life has a way of giving us little bits of hope when we need them most; you just have to be open to seeing and appreciating them. When I choose *hope* as my word, I find I am more aware of everything in life that gives me hope. Hope in nature. Hope in myself. Hope in my community. And hope in my world.

Of course, there will always be times when those little bits of hope aren't enough, times when circumstances feel so dark and so heavy that nothing can cut through the gloom. When hope is in short supply, I place my hope squarely in something far bigger than myself—God. When things are at their worst and I feel anxiety rear its ugly head, I can pray and share all of my worries, stressors, and feelings, and suddenly my

flame of hope burns brighter and stronger. It is always a mighty relief to hand my problems over to God. I know there's nothing He can't handle, and that truth gives me rest and helps me find peace even when life is chaotic. So if you find yourself losing hope, try praying, even if it's not something you do often (or ever), and even if you feel like no one is listening. Turning to the Higher Power you believe in is a beautiful, relieving way to build up the hope in your heart.

Another trick I have for reclaiming hope when things feel hopeless is to take a purposeful pause from working on, talking about, or even thinking about the hopeless situation. Try writing out the situation on paper—and include every detail, no matter how shameful, embarrassing, or grim. Let yourself sit there and fully feel the feelings that come along with the situation. Then tuck the paper away, and give yourself at least a night off (although I take a few days off, if I can) from your worries. I know it sounds counterproductive, especially when the situation is urgent, but this will allow you to rest

Yes, my soul, find rest in God; my hope comes from him.

—PSALM 62:5

EVERY WORD MATTERS

and come back to the paper with fresh eyes. You can then look for places where even a small change would give you hope, small places you couldn't easily spot when consumed with hopelessness.

If you try this exercise and still don't see anything after a good break, take the paper to someone you trust and let her suggest changes or ideas you may have missed. When we're deep in the woods, all we can see are trees. Someone outside of the woods can see what you've been missing—a clearing, an easier trail, or even the way out.

IN GOOD TIMES AND BAD

We talk the most about hope when we're going through afflictions, but that's not the only time we should embrace the notion. Hope can make difficult circumstances more bearable, but it can also help improve our lives at any time. The very act of hoping for better things can motivate us to take actions to lean into our higher self and to make those things real. When we have hope, we have a spark of faith that we can succeed, making us more patient, resilient, determined, and courageous. We need hope

WAYS TO BOOST HOPE

- Close your eyes, take a few deep breaths, and meditate on all the possibilities your life could bring.

- Rest. Sometimes lying in the grass under a big, life-giving tree, sipping a big glass of water, and getting a good night's sleep can give you back that glimmer of hope you've been missing.

- Pray. God is so much bigger than we are. Trust Him to steer. Get quiet to listen for His voice.

- Focus on the positive. Write down three hopeful things that happened to you at the end of each day.

- Clarify. Write down what you are hoping for, and say it out loud each morning.

- Celebrate small wins and big wins alike. When times are tough, an extra piece of cake or two certainly can't hurt!

— Humble yourself to reach out for support. Call on your friends, family, neighbors, and anyone else in your community that you can. We were never ever meant to walk through dark times alone. It takes a village.

— See a therapist, see a counselor, or find a support group to attend. There is a wide range of therapy options in all budgets these days, and working with a good therapist can supercharge your hope. There are free twelve-step programs for pretty much every issue under the sun. These aren't just for addiction issues anymore—they're also for codependence, debt, love and sex struggles, food issues, etc. (I used to attend a few in person, but now I go to some via Zoom and love to start my day off listening to them while I walk or run around my neighborhood.)

Change your thoughts and you change your world.

—NORMAN VINCENT PEALE

when we are facing uncertainties—even exciting ones like graduating from school, starting a new job, having our first baby, or getting married. Anytime we step into something new, we do so with a measure of hope that it will be a success; otherwise, we'd never be willing to change anything or take a risk. Hope is really the first step of any endeavor.

Hope is much more than a simple wish. It's the active belief that something will come to be. I also believe that hope is something that can be cultivated and that we can intentionally make ourselves more hopeful. Every single world-changer throughout history has been hopeful. They've had to hope in the future, hope in their ideas, and hope they could make things better before they could begin to make a difference. Hope can be a choice, a limitless attitude walking hand in hand with the creativity and hard work needed to turn hope into reality.

CHOOSING HOPE

If you approach every situation with intentional hope, with the confident expectation that it will ultimately turn out well in the long run,

then you'll start to clearly see how everything turns out the way it was always meant to. Not every situation will go perfectly, of course, but instead of focusing on all the ways it didn't work out, you'll be more likely to notice and celebrate even the smallest successes. You'll be encouraged by the little wins pointing the way to your bigger goals. Your hope will keep you moving forward even when there are setbacks and even when no one around you sees the possibilities that you do.

So how can we cultivate hope in our hearts when it doesn't come naturally? I've been there. Sometimes it feels impossible. Being hopeful is so much more than being positive and optimistic. To be honest, I'm not a naturally optimistic, glass-half-full type of person, but I've done deep work over the years to train my brain to go in a different direction. I've cultivated hope. I've gone through many periods in my life when I wasn't terribly hopeful. It took work to relight that spark of hope in my heart, and it took work to stoke it into a cheerful fire.

So much of it, for me, is noticing and acknowledging everything I have to be hopeful about. Write out a list of all of the good, hope-inspiring things (including people) in your life. This isn't just a list of things you are thankful for—I can be thankful for my twenty-year-old car and abandon hope that it's going to keep running for much longer, right? This list should be people and things that really do inspire hope in your heart. Look at it often and add to it. I want to challenge you to say three things out loud to yourself every day that you are hopeful about. Say them with conviction to yourself in the morning before you start your day and at night right before you go to bed.

The point is to train your brain to focus on hope rather than on despair. To see the possibilities in front of you instead of seeing only improbabilities. Try setting a specific goal for something you hope for, either something internally or emotionally, or something outside of yourself. Chart out the steps it will take you to get there, and focus on making progress each day, no matter how small. Think ahead to obstacles you might encounter and how to overcome them, so that when you do hit a speed bump, you will feel hopeful navigating it. Over time you will find yourself feeling hopeful about your goals and more hopeful about your life in general. When you cultivate a hopeful attitude, you are choosing to hope over and over, despite the odds. And isn't that a beautiful choice to make?

Live life as if
everything
is rigged in
your favor.

—RUMI

Reflect

I want to leave you with questions to journal about, discuss with a trusted friend, or reflect on. These are the same questions I ask myself when I am desperate for hope.

When I feel hopeful, how does it affect my daily actions?

_____

_____

_____

What have I felt most hopeful about lately?

_____

_____

What have I felt the least hopeful about lately? How can I alter how I feel about these circumstances?

_____

_____

_____

_____

_____

What can I do to boost hope in every situation?

_____

_____

_____

_____

SEVEN

What you say and do and share has the power to inspire, impact, and heal others' hearts. When you choose *inspire* as your word, you are committing to get inspired and then to share your unique story and your thoughts to inspire others. Meditating on this word is about reminding yourself that you have love and wisdom to share with the people in your life, both the ones you see every day and the ones you might connect with via social media or other outlets all over the world. Think about how you feel when you connect with someone's story and it leaves a tangible mark on your life. What if you could do the same for someone else? There is someone out there who *needs* to hear what you have to say, so let's get inspired and start sharing!

If you don't feel terribly inspired, then it can feel daunting to just up and go find inspiration. Don't worry; choosing *inspire* as your word doesn't mean you have to be 100 percent inspired all the time. There will be days when you are bursting with ideas and energy, and days when the only thing you feel inspired to do is pour yourself another cup of coffee. But even on your most blah days, there are things you can do to feel more motivated about this quest. The trick is to get into the habit of prioritizing these practices in your day-to-day routine so you spend more time inspired than not.

Think about when you feel the most inspired. What are you doing? Where are you? How do you feel? I'm often inspired at night, when I'm alone and can really connect with my thoughts. That's when I used to write my favorite gut-wrenching songs and draw design sketches. But I'm always most inspired when dealing with some sort of hardship. When I, someone I know, or the world in general is facing something traumatic or difficult, it motivates me to come up with solutions. I'm inspired when I'm connecting to a need I can see and feel. It motivates me to pursue my purpose with abandon. For you, it may be getting up early each morning to watch the sunrise and journal or read a book that

I've learned that people will forget what you said, people will forget what you did, but people will never forget how you made them feel.

—MAYA ANGELOU

stimulates your imagination. Or it might be taking a full day each weekend to go for long walks or connect with friends who really motivate you to dream bigger. Try a few different things and see which one really gets your brain and heart going.

WHO ARE YOU INSPIRING?

We all have so much untapped potential just lying dormant, waiting to make a lasting impact on those around us. We choose each day whether we want to inspire and lift one another up, or whether we want to focus only on ourselves or waste our energy cutting one another down. Think about this as you find yourself scrolling through social media—do the accounts you follow make you feel horrible about yourself and your life, or do they fill you with joy and excitement? Are you getting ideas from what you see, or are you scrolling mindlessly to numb out? Have you gotten yourself into an online fight in the comments section? It's happened to the best of us. Why do we find ourselves in this place from time to time?

WAYS TO FUEL INSPIRATION

— Spend time in nature. Go for a walk or a challenging hike, have a picnic in the park, or even dine al fresco in your own backyard for a few nights. Let the beauty of the natural world sink in.

— Try something new. Always wanted to take a ballet class, but were sure you had two left feet? Today's the day! Learning a new skill will help shake up your routine. And you never know—all those pirouettes may shake loose a great new idea in your brain too!

— Lean into the arts. Head to a local museum for the day, get tickets to the symphony, go see a play, or visit a local pottery studio to get your hands dirty. Art doesn't happen without inspiration, so let someone else's work inspire yours.

— Be of service. Volunteer with an organization to actively help others in your community. Helping others is like an energy drink for the soul. Seeing good be done and hearing the stories of people I'm helping always gets me in an inspired mood.

Refresh your space. Clean out your clutter, rearrange your furniture, hang up new pictures, pick up a few plants, or even paint a room a new color. We spend a lot of time in our homes. If yours isn't an inspiring place to be, it's time to change that. Even if you don't have the budget to make big changes, at the very least create a space in your home for you to do the inspired work you are trying to do.

Rest. If you are feeling utterly depleted, it's time to up your sleeping game. Go to bed early for a few nights, and try to sleep for at least eight hours. So few of us actually get the quality rest we need, so it's no wonder if you are feeling decidedly uninspired. Make rest a priority, and you'll be shocked at what it can do for your ability to think clearly.

Read a good book. Think about which books you've read that have really captured your imagination or made you feel deeply. Reread those! Or take yourself to your local bookstore or library (to actually *smell* the depth of the history in the pages and give your eyes a break from reading on tech devices), and ask for new recommendations that are similar to old favorites. Make sure to share what felt so inspiring to you with the salesclerk or librarian so they can help you find books that will really work for you.

We've fallen into the trap of pride, rage, judgmental hatred, and comparison. Instead of cheering on one another (or kindly and respectfully sharing our opposing opinion), we find ourselves comparing our own unique, wonderfully imperfect, wild, and, yes, messy lives with the top-level, different perspectives and perfectly polished highlight reels that someone else is showing the world. Deep down in our hearts, we know those snapshots aren't the whole story. We know that between the photos posted of luxurious, tropical vacations and adorable kids in matching outfits, there are millions of moments we don't see—burned dinners, failed health and businesses, tantrums, anxiety, blowout fights, loneliness, antidepressants, and scrubbing toilets. Everyone's life is messy and emotional and a roller-coaster of highs and lows. That's what it is to be human. None of us is perfect. So how do we stop comparing and start connecting? That's where *inspire* comes in.

The opposite of comparison isn't just not to compare; it's to inspire. Comparison is all about looking for similarities and differences and then making judgments based on those. When you inspire, you aren't doling out judgment; you're sharing celebration. You look closer and really *see* everyone else, and then celebrate what about them inspires you. And, in turn, you are sharing your most authentic self instead of hiding behind your own facade—which will then inspire others.

No one is perfect. In fact, I think we are all drawn to people who own their imperfections and don't try to smile through the struggle to hide them. We like them because they give us permission to be imperfect ourselves. So let it all hang out: the good, the bad, and the beautifully flawed and so-called ugly. Once you start to feel the ideas, life, passion, and inspiration, you can better focus on your work, your art, and expressing yourself just as you are—imperfections and all—and comparison just sort of falls away. Inspired people inspire people.

INSPIRATION SQUAD

In that spirit, I want to encourage you to surround yourself with friends and mentors who challenge and inspire you. The more people around you who make you think, warm your heart, and encourage you to be your highest, most creative self, the more inspired and inspiring you will be. It's a ripple effect. Actively seek out those people. You may already be a part of a vibrant community like that. But if you aren't, there's no time like the present to start building that community for yourself.

Think of your three most inspiring friends, and invite them all out

WAYS TO INSPIRE OTHERS

- Lead with humility.
- Do less talking and more active listening and seeing. Notice what people are *really* saying and feeling beneath the surface.
- Lead with empathy. Slow down, and let your heart break for all the pain you see around you. Dream up ways to meet those needs.
- Add a "give back" component to your business or household.
- Start posting mostly inspirational content.
- Leave an anonymous encouraging note on someone's car.
- Buy coffee for the person behind you in line.

to brunch, whether they know one another or not. Tell them why they inspire you and why you think they may inspire one another. Then share with them what you're focusing on, be it at work, in your larger community, or even just within yourself. Ask for their input, and then ask how you can help them with the inspirational work they are doing. Special things happen when we humble ourselves, unite, and work together.

Hopefully your little group will be equally encouraged, and you can make Inspiration Brunches a *thing* that you do regularly. If not, don't give up. Try a different group next weekend, and do it until you find the right mix of people who really rev one another up! Schedule regular time to meet with these people, and add more inspiring folks to the mix as you go. This is the group, more than any other, that will help you accomplish all the big things you've been dreaming of.

Take the same approach when it comes to social media. How many different people are you following? How do their posts make you feel? When they come up in your feed, are you excited to see what they've been up to? Or do you cringe a little, knowing those posts will make you feel less than? It's time for a little social media spring cleaning!

This may take you a while, depending on how many people you

follow, but try to go through ten to twenty accounts a day. (This is an excellent activity for killing time while you are waiting for takeout, sitting on the loo, or standing in a line.) Look at their feeds and stories, and assess how you feel. If you don't feel inspired or, at the very least, positive about what you see, consider unfollowing. If they make you feel less-than, angry, small, jealous, or depressed about yourself and your life, unfollow immediately. I don't care if it's a popular influencer, a company whose product you genuinely like, your best friend, your easily offended coworker, or even a family member. You don't need that kind of negativity taking up residence in your mind or your heart.

> # Comparison is an act of violence against the self.
>
> —IYANLA VANZANT

It may feel strange to unfollow someone, especially if they are someone you know personally, but we all need to stop consuming content that invites negativity and comparison and, instead, feed our eyes and hearts with inspiring content that helps us see the truth about our unique identity and purpose in life. And if every account bums you out, then it's time for a social media detox. Delete those apps from your phone, and take a few weeks or months off. You'll be amazed at the time you get back that you were spending looking at other people's lives instead of focusing on really living your own.

FEED YOUR PURPOSE

We all have a unique purpose, something that lights us up inside and makes life so much sweeter. But even when you are pursuing purpose with everything you've got, it's still possible to get discouraged, jaded, and just plain ol' burned out if you don't keep your inspiration tank full.

I love what I do at The Giving Keys and how it feeds into my purpose of encouraging women to embrace and love their flaws, but sometimes it is really challenging. I can't tell you how many days I've cried on the way to work, during meetings, on phone calls, and on the way home again at night. I didn't go to business school or plan to be a CEO, and there's no manual out there for employing people trying to transition out of homelessness who may be dealing with abusive

HOW TO INSPIRE ON SOCIAL MEDIA

- Be kind always.
- Pull back the curtain on your highlight reel, and share more from your real life.
- Forget being perfect; instead, be authentic.
- Stand up for yourself and others, but know when to walk away from trolls and bullies.
- Consider your content. How is what you are posting inspiring or helping others? Are you creating content just for content's sake or to convey an important message?
- Scrub the list of influencers you follow. If an account doesn't inspire you, unfollow. If an account makes you feel less than or jealous, unfollow. If an account makes you second-guess your choices, intuition, or sanity, unfollow.

situations, addiction, and unresolved trauma. I have given my all to my company, sometimes to the exclusion of everything else in my life. But when I'm not staying inspired, my all isn't worth that much. I've learned that it is imperative for me to take time to get and stay inspired, no matter how many other urgent things are on my to-do list. When I lose my inspiration, I stop being able to inspire my team and my customers—and then we all lose.

I promise that staying inspired is imperative for you too. You may not be the CEO of a small business, but I guarantee there are people around you who look up to you and are inspired by what you do. You have a purpose that you were created to find and dive into, the work of a lifetime that needs you to be on fire with inspiration and passion. This doesn't even have to be a career or movement you start; it can be being a mother too. Being a mother is the hardest, most exhausting (yet most fulfilling) job I've ever had. Take the time to find your personal well of inspiration. Shore it up, brick by brick, with your habits and priorities, and then you can draw from it every day. If you can do that, there's really nothing you can't accomplish.

Reflect

I want to leave you with questions to journal about, discuss with a trusted friend, or reflect on. These are the same questions I ask myself when I want to inspire.

When, in the past, have you felt the most inspired? Why do you think that was?

_____

What were you doing then that you might not be doing now?

_____

Name every person in your life who inspires you and why.

_____

Which of these people do you think would
inspire one another the most?

_____

_____

_____

How can you bring them together to
build an Inspiration Squad?

_____

_____

What else can you do to add inspiration to your life?

_____

_____

EIGHT

Create is such a beautiful, freeing, colorful, juicy, fabulous, bold, exciting word! I can't think of another word that is so filled with possibility. For me, it's about being free. When I focus on *create*, I allow myself to meander and take my time, eyes opened wide to drink in the colors, sounds, and unique intricacies of my life. I look for what sets my soul ablaze with beauty, and let that guide me to dance, paint, sing, write, and generally pour myself into something special.

Even if you don't feel like a traditionally creative person, you still have the power to create with your words, your body, and your actions. As you go through your days, you are radiating life and energy into the world that can create a powerful ripple effect. Only *you* can create that particular ripple. I have seen people benefit the most from focusing on *create* when they harness freedom and energy and use it to make something new. That's what *create* is all about—opening up your heart and then following where it leads. This is the word to pick if you are feeling stuck, down, or low on energy. This is the word that will shake you up and help you see the world around you differently.

FIND YOUR VOICE

Not surprisingly, I consider myself a creative person. I was an actor and singer-songwriter-musician for much of my career. But finding my own voice and using that to channel my creativity wasn't something that happened overnight. In my younger years, I was a part of a girl band that had been signed to Arista Records under Kenny "Babyface" Edmonds. He is a truly inspired songwriter, producer, and performer who has worked with everyone from Whitney Houston to Mariah Carey to Eric Clapton to P!nk. He was one of the first people to look at the very basic songs I was writing and see potential in them. He didn't dismiss me just

because the topics I wanted to write about weren't exactly mainstream. (At the time, pop stars weren't writing about homelessness, God, and finding contentment instead of fame.) He really encouraged me to listen to my inner voice and reach harder and wider to write from the heart. He always pushed me to try to make the lyrics more "clever," which still sticks in my mind today when I'm creating products and marketing campaigns for The Giving Keys.

When I left that group, I went back to college and continued acting. Later, I began to work on music of my own, and Babyface signed me as a solo artist. He believed there was room out there for the messages I wanted to share, so he took a chance and gave me a platform so that I could dig deep and create songs from my unique perspective. The world needs to hear and see what you can create from your story, heart, and mind too.

YOU HAVE WHAT IT TAKES

Create is a word that can stop people right in their tracks. They will look at it, shake their heads, and say, "Create? Not for me! I'm not creative at all." It's sad to hear anyone say that because I truly believe we are all creative. I know when many people think about creativity, they picture art, music, dance, or even crafts (I am hopeless at crafts!), but those are certainly not the only ways to create.

Everyone's creativity shows up in different ways. Like me, you may not be big on crafts, but perhaps you are a brilliant creative strategist in the boardroom. The thought of performing in public may give you chills, but perhaps you delight friends and family with your delicious culinary creations. Or maybe you simply want to focus on creating a life you love. My creativity won't look like yours, and what you create will be something I could never do, and that's what makes it all so wonderful! I think many of us get so wrapped up in what creativity is *supposed* to look like that we forget to look around and see what it actually is for each of us as individuals.

Don't feel pressured to start with *create* by penning a song or painting a masterpiece. There are tons of small ways to incorporate this word into your everyday life. You never know where little creative steps may take you. When I pulled a battered brass key out of my bag and slipped it onto a chain around my neck, I had no idea that I had just taken my first

step toward The Giving Keys. I'm certainly not the first person to create key jewelry, but if I hadn't been willing to create something, I would have missed out on an incredible journey. Hear me when I say this: You are every bit as magical and creative as anyone else. Others may have created similar art, stories, marketing plans, whatever else you put your heart into—but no one has your unique voice and creativity.

Saying "I'm not creative" is just an excuse we tell ourselves because we are pigeonholing our abilities into a too-small box when we're afraid we'll fail. We're afraid our painting will look like something a toddler made. (I call it abstract!) We're afraid we'll sing flat notes through our entire song. We're afraid our masterpiece will be deemed mediocre. But that fear is holding us back and keeping us trapped in safe little boxes without much room for growth. We're not going to make an impact on the world inside a box.

Every woman out there changing industries, shaking up culture, and making a difference has something in common: They've all seen problems as opportunities for something new and maybe a little wild. Those special ideas, the world-changing ones, are always outside of the box. That doesn't mean that those women have gotten it right the first

GET IN A CREATIVE SPACE

↝ **FIND A UNIQUE JOURNAL AND START WRITING.** Write about your day, what you saw and discovered, what you're grateful for, ideas you have, or even questions you're struggling with. Writing every day will help you tap into your inner writer.

↝ **LEARN SOMETHING NEW.** Challenge yourself to acquire a new skill. Whether you want to master Photoshop or learn how to cook a meal other than a box of mac 'n cheese, the process of learning and practicing something new and challenging will get your creative juices flowing.

↝ **UPCYCLE.** Breathe new life into something old and drab. Revive a hand-me-down piece of furniture that needs some TLC with chalkboard paint. Give a dated mirror or picture frame a coat of gold spray paint. Or even take a page from my book and turn an old ring, key, or random small home device or tool into a necklace or key chain!

— **EMBRACE NATURE.** Get outside and get your hands in the dirt. Plant flowers by your front door, or a place a pot of succulents on your coffee table. Even a little pot of herbs for your kitchen windowsill will breathe new life into your daily routine.

— **GET BUSY IN THE KITCHEN.** Pick a recipe you've been dying to try, review it, and then give it your own twist. Add a few extra ingredients or try a different sauce. You may end up with an inedible mess, but more likely you'll have found a great new dish tailored to your tastes!

time—or even the hundredth time—but they have been willing to try and fail, pivot, rework things, and improve as they go. They didn't give up on creating just because they weren't good at it right out of the gate. That means you don't have to give up either!

Think about the millions of people in this world who have ideas bubbling inside, just waiting to be acted upon. That untapped potential is pure gold. Why aren't more of us mining for it? What are we missing out on in this world because you're telling yourself that you aren't creative? Start now. Start small. Get creative in a way that only unique *you* can.

MAKE THE CHOICE

One of the best ways you can get started is to make emotional space and time for creativity, just like you would for anything else that's important to you. But don't try to shoehorn creative thinking into the fringes of each day. Instead, choose the time of day when you are most naturally creative. I don't do my best creative work in the middle of the day with dozens of people vying for my attention. I have to save time when I can be alone with my thoughts and no one will interrupt me.

Take a break, and go on a walk so you can inhale some deep breaths and see all the life happening around you. For me, sometimes my creative time is at night or very early in the morning when my husband and babies are sleeping peacefully. It might feel silly to sit down and create at a dedicated time, and your first few attempts may all be throwaways. But over time you'll feel more and more comfortable, and your creative work will improve. The space and work between an idea and something new that wows the world, or just your soul alone, is what *create* is all about. So make the time to do the work.

Need another way to jump-start your creativity? Find a creative community to call your own! Even if you happen to be a successful creative genius, I promise you will benefit from working with other creative geniuses. You may find that your projects plus their projects equals something unlike anything the world has ever seen before, something new and exciting that could be life-changing. It could lead you to your next job, help you find the business partner you never knew you needed, or even help you meet a new lifelong friend. Collaborating can have a bigger impact that inspires others to create too. When you are free with your talents and willing to share them with others, you will find that others feel more creative and willing to share their talents too. And that's how creative revolutions are made!

Choosing *create* as a focus means choosing freedom. It's choosing freedom from the fear of failure, freedom from the box you've been hiding in, and freedom to run full force after the ideas you are passionate about. That freedom is waiting for you, so go claim it.

EVERY WORD MATTERS

Reflect

I want to leave you with questions to journal about, discuss with a trusted friend, or reflect on. These are the same questions I ask myself when I lean in to create.

What makes your heart come alive? What is the one thing you love doing, thinking about, or learning about the most?

_____

_____

_____

What are you usually doing when you get your best ideas? Are you on your morning run? Right in the middle of a hot shower?

A café? Staring at an ocean or mountains? Or are you sitting at your desk with a pen in hand ready to jot down ideas?

_____

_____

_____

Is there something you've always wanted to do but haven't? You know the thing I'm talking about: the thing you always promise yourself you'll start on as soon as your schedule isn't quite so busy or as soon as you finally get that promotion at work. Write it down here, and make a commitment to make time for it.

_____

_____

_____

NINE

Let's talk about fear. The biggest barrier between what we *really want* to say, do, and be and what we *actually* say, do, and become is fear—the fear that we won't be enough for the job, the fear of our own voices, and the fear that we will fail or be embarrassed. I think there is a point in each of our lives, usually when we are still kids, when we think to be *brave* means to have no fear. We want to be brave because we want to escape from fear. But the more we live, the more we realize that being brave means taking fear's hand and making it our friend, dragging it along with us while we say, do, and become those things we want anyway.

We named our son Brave. We wanted him to have a name that

would equip him to be bold and confident. Being brave means you're ready to face the hard things, even when they're scary. It means you will walk in your courage to stand up for what you believe in. You will stand up for what is right. You will climb that mountain. You will face your fears. You will fall and get back up again. You will be resilient.

SCARY GOOD

How would being brave change your life? What would you do if you knew you couldn't fail? Which dreams would you go for if you knew you wouldn't be embarrassed or shamed? You probably have a list. If you don't, make one, and then come back to this chapter. What's the easiest thing to tackle on the list? The hardest? The quickest? Start with whichever. You can dip your toe into *brave* or dive in headfirst. *Geronimo!*

Certain things in life are just easier to go along with. It's easier to stay in a job you're good at but tolerate than to face your fear that says, "This is the best you'll ever do" and take the leap to pursue a new career.

**The best way
out is always
through.**

—ROBERT FROST

It's easier to end relationships than it is to face your fear of getting your heart broken or do the deep work of trekking through the painful mud to get to the other side. It's easier to change the channel when the news shows an injustice that breaks your heart, makes you feel helpless, and nudges you to action than it is to look for ways to help and then actually do them.

This, to me, is the definition of not tapping into your fullest potential and resolving yourself to living dim and small. Have you ever gone bowling with a child? They'll put bumpers up so when the ball tries to go into the gutter, it is bounced back into the lane to hit the pins. Living small is living life with bumpers. Boy, do I have news for you. If you can be brave enough to set aside those bumpers, you'll find yourself with your pick of lanes, all with shiny, sparkling, new pins to knock down.

FEAR LIES

Our fears scream so loud at us, spitting out lies with just enough truth buried in them to make them believable. They'll tell you it's just too hard. (It *will* be hard, but that doesn't mean you aren't capable of doing it!) They'll tell you it'll be too embarrassing to take a public risk. (You might feel embarrassed or uncomfortable, but once you take those first few steps, you'll begin to feel confident and strong!)

Your fears will tell you *anything* they have to in order to keep you right where you are. But there are so many opportunities waiting for you on the other side of your fears. That's where *brave* comes in. *Brave* helps you choose the good thing you can't see *yet* over the lies your fears want you to believe. It's time to start living big, walking in the truth that you can overcome fear, and deciding you're brave enough to do it.

FACE IT

When we bump up against a fear, many of us are usually quick to push away from it, drop the dream, and forget that it even existed. Our minds are so skilled at distracting us from our fears that you may not even realize what your fear is, let alone how to overcome it. So how do you work through a fear you don't even know you have?

Remember that list we talked about earlier? Go back to it when you have time to be alone. Pick the first dream on your list, and close your eyes. Take several deep breaths from your belly until you feel yourself relax. Now picture that dream in your mind. See yourself doing the work to make it real. See yourself accomplishing the dream. Now picture yourself going for that dream . . . and failing to make it work out. As you imagine, pay attention to your body. Did something you pictured make your heart beat a little faster? Did you feel your muscles tense? Did you have the urge to open your eyes and stop imagining? Congrats! You bumped up against a fear.

Go back to the moment in your imagination that made your body respond. What were you doing? Were you imagining announcing to friends and family that you are going after your dream? You might have a fear of embarrassment. Were you doing something

> **One of the greatest discoveries a man makes, one of his great surprises, is to find he can do what he was afraid he couldn't do.**
>
> —HENRY FORD

risky and out of character? You might have a fear of change. Were you messing up? Fear of failure. Were you doing something you've never done before? Fear of the unknown. Whatever it is, try to name that fear. Call it like you see it, and write it down on your list.

FEEL IT ALL

When people talk about overcoming their fears, I always picture them leaping over their fears like they are doing the pole vault at the Olympics. But the truth is, there is no way to leap, skip, or jump over your fears. Really, the only way out is through. If you want to stop living small, you must allow yourself to *feel* the fear instead of suppressing it. Committing to *brave* means committing to face your giants because you know deep down you can.

Once you can identify your fears, you can start to feel them. A huge part of this process is being intentional and mindful. When you start to feel those fear feelings, be brave and hold onto them; let yourself fully feel them. Let the worst that fear can dish out wash over you. Cry if you need to. Scream if it helps. Go for a run if you have the urge to flee. But don't let those fear feelings go. You'll know when you've pushed through to the other side; you'll feel it deeply in your heart and in your spirit. High-five!

Of course, this doesn't mean your fear is gone. It just means that you know you can live through it. You'll know that feeling fear isn't nearly as bad as living small is. So when you come up against that fear again, you'll be ready. You'll be brave and feel your way through it again.

Once you get comfortable with feeling your fear, you will come to appreciate it when you hit a fear bumper. It will let you know that you are on the right track, that you are being brave and going for what you really want. Fear will become a friend you bring along for the ride as your life gets bigger, bolder, and braver every time you meet.

You can do hard things! You've done them before and you will do them again. Life gives plenty of opportunities for do-overs. No one is immune to fear, but having the bravery to push past fear to accomplish something that matters will give you a boost of confidence like nothing else.

Reflect

I want to leave you with questions to journal about, discuss
with a trusted friend, or reflect on. These are the same questions I ask myself when I embrace being brave.

What is your biggest emotional fear?

_____

_____

_____

_____

_____

_____

Why is that so frightening to you?

_____

_____

_____

_____

_____

What would be a simple step you could
take to start facing that fear?

_____

_____

_____

_____

TEN

Strength has always been The Giving Keys' top-selling word. It's so interesting because it shows that strength is what most people feel they need most. And I get it. I think most people feel weak and out of control in the face of the pain and hardships that inevitably come our way. We all hope that we have a well of strength deep enough to not only get us through hard times, but to also allow us to emerge triumphantly with our heads held high with resilient confidence. Choosing *strength* as your word can help you find and nurture your own strength and remind you that you are strong when you forget.

WEAK AND STRONG

Let's face it: Life can and will be difficult at times. If we are being truly honest with ourselves, none of us have very much control over the waves that life will wash over us. Natural disasters, diseases, and economic downturns affect us all, young and old, rich and poor, powerless and powerful. So much of our circumstances depends on luck or fate or just being in the wrong place at the wrong time. And yet our culture tells us that only the strong survive. That if you fail to recover from a difficult situation, you are weak and have only yourself to blame. And that the weak are expendable. It's no wonder we all want more strength!

The truth is that all of us are weak, and all of us are strong. Our weaknesses don't all look the same and neither do our strengths. If we listen only to our culture, we might think that strength only looks a certain way: someone who never shows emotion, who never backs down, who goes down fighting. Someone who grins and bears it when things are bad, who grits her teeth and keeps going, even if she's exhausted and bleeding. And, yes, that is absolutely what strength looks like sometimes.

Any action is often better than no action, especially if you have been stuck in an unhappy situation for a long time. If it is a mistake, at least you learn something, in which case it's no longer a mistake. If you remain stuck, you learn nothing.

—ECKHART TOLLE

But strength can also look a lot like weakness by that (limited) definition. It can look like someone crying and grieving as she makes a difficult decision. It can be someone who surrenders instead of fights, because that is the *only* way through. It can be asking for help or choosing to rest so you can live to fight another day. It can be whispering prayers instead of throwing punches.

I know that one of my biggest strengths is my ability to emotionally connect with others. That means I cry as easily as I laugh (including in meetings at my company!). Some people might see that as a weakness, but I don't. I feel strong when I can stay open and vulnerable when I hear the difficult stories of some of my employees transitioning out of homelessness and the stories of The Giving Keys' customers. So many of those stories include devastating addictions, trauma, disease, and profound loss. I've seen some people shut down, unable to fully engage because of how uncomfortable those stories made them. But I believe I was made to stay right there, holding hands and really hearing and seeing their pain. Those aren't traditional strengths, and it took me a while to see them for what they truly are, but now I know they are my superpowers. What are yours?

I AM STRONG

It can be easy to mistake strength for weakness when we are struggling our way through a horrible situation or trying to bounce back from a devastating loss. When we are in pain or working through trauma, it's almost impossible to see ourselves accurately without a little help. There is a season for everything. There is a season to grieve and to rest in that place. And there is a season to stand up, dust yourself off, and get back on the horse (so to speak). That is where your focus on strength can really help.

One of my favorite limited collections we have created at The Giving Keys was the I Am collection. Each piece of jewelry in the collection included a set of two keys. One key said *I Am* and the other had various words such as *brave, fearless, strong,* and *loved*. When we received the first samples, our marketing director asked which word I wanted. I immediately reached for the *I Am Strong* necklace. I'd been really struggling with some emotionally charged business decisions, and I felt like I was constantly near tears. I felt like strength was in desperately short supply. She smiled and nodded and said, "Oh, that's perfect for you because you are *so* strong!" I was shocked, and I admitted that I wanted that necklace because I felt so weak. She looked at me like I had lost it. She could see that I already had the strength I was longing for. I'd just forgotten that it was there.

In that moment, I realized I'd been believing and repeating a lie about myself and letting it keep me small. I hadn't been walking in the truth that I am strong. I needed to change the narrative I was telling myself. So I took the time to sit down and write out a list of all the things that prove I am strong. My story is a story of strength and resilience; I just needed to remind myself of that. It was time to walk tall in my strength. I needed to believe it. I needed to champion myself. I wore my *I Am Strong* necklace as a reminder that I am strong even when I don't feel like it.

BELIEVE IN YOUR STRENGTH

The words we use to describe ourselves shape our beliefs about our abilities. We become what we believe. So start practicing believing you are

We are not necessarily doubting that God will do the best for us; we are wondering how painful the best will turn out to be.

—C. S. LEWIS

strong, brave, fearless, and loved. Train yourself to believe the best about yourself, and that's exactly what you will become. Having trouble *feeling* that belief, truly believing you are strong?

Think about activities and hobbies that make you feel strong. Maybe it's taking a challenging kickboxing class or volunteering at your favorite organization or going for a long run. Maybe it's having lunch with a friend who has a knack for building you up or calling your mom for a pep talk or even organizing your closet. Whatever those things are for you, it's time to begin prioritizing those activities. Write them into your planner every week, and don't let yourself skip them. The more often you feel strong, the more confident you'll become in your own strength.

I want to challenge you to make your own list of all the ways you embody strength. Think through all the times you've overcome difficulties, all the times you stood up for yourself and others, all the times you didn't give up when it would have been easier to let something important within you die. Write all of that down.

Now think through all of the things about yourself that make you feel weak. Are you sure those are weaknesses? Maybe you feel weak because you avoid confrontation and arguments, but doesn't it take an awful lot of strength not to take the bait and instead wait until everyone has calmed down to talk? Or maybe you think your emotional responses are a weakness? I'd argue that it takes true strength to allow yourself to *really* feel your feelings and work through them instead of shoving them down because they are too scary.

Take a break, and then look at your list again with an objective eye or ask a trusted friend to look with you. I bet you have way more strengths than you realized. Make a revised list and look at it anytime you feel your strength flagging.

LOOK UP

Of course, you don't have to face life's difficulties alone. There are some situations that no one has enough strength to get through. When I find myself staring down a dark night and I can feel that my well won't be nearly enough to get me through, I turn to God, who is the Source of the strength I can't muster up with my own broken, human abilities. When

I pray and trust God to help me, He soothes and fills my well, and I find I can get through another day. One day at a time.

Don't hesitate to reach out to God when you need a dose of strength, big or small. It's never a weakness to call for help when you need it.

MINDFUL STRENGTH

While none of us can control what the future holds, we can control how we respond to any given situation. We can react blindly, let our worries and anxieties lead us to fumble our way through. Or we can choose to be intentional and mindfully approach issues. Part of being strong is being strategic, taking control of your thoughts, thinking rationally and clearly, and giving yourself time and space to process your feelings even if you feel overwhelmed.

When you're living in the mistakes and failures and messes that happened yesterday or predicting that horrible things might happen next week, you aren't focusing on what's right in front of you. When you're going through a difficult time, it is important to let yourself feel it, and then stay in the moment and not let your mind run away with you into doom and gloomsville. If you don't, you risk missing out on the sweet, savory good things right in front of you, like valuable information that could help with your current situation, the support of friends, or chances for laughter and joy. You can't change the past, and you can deal with the future only when you get there, so don't let all of the what-ifs control you. If you must, allow yourself a set amount of time each day to think through possibilities and solutions for the future. Once that time is over, set those thoughts aside.

Big emotions always accompany the tough stuff in life. Living in denial doesn't do you any favors. If at all possible, slow down. Cancel some commitments, and make room in your schedule to deal with your feelings. That may mean taking a long bubble bath, or letting yourself cry for a while, or making an appointment with a professional counselor to talk through what's weighing on your heart and mind. Whatever works for you, prioritize it. This will help you think more clearly and give you the precious emotional bandwidth you need to be able to handle whatever life throws at you.

STRONGER THAN EVER

No matter how strong you are, there will be times that test your strength. That's just how life is. Though going through these periods can feel like we're stuck in a black cloud of torture, what I've found is the times that have most tested my strength are the times that have helped make me a better version of myself. The situations that make us choose *strength* as our word are the same situations that stretch us, that show us what's most important in life, that help us find our purpose, that show us how much we are truly capable of, and that teach us the lessons we need to be successful in the long run.

That's true of my friends too. The women I love and admire most for their poise and resilience didn't get to be that way because everything worked out for them. They got that way because hard things happened and they learned how to deal with them, to find their strength and flex it, to keep going until they came out the other side stronger than ever. You can be one of those women too, and I'm willing to bet you already are!

Reflect

I want to leave you with questions to journal about, discuss with a trusted friend, or reflect on. These are the same questions I ask myself when I need to remind myself of my strength.

When have you felt the strongest? Why?

_____

_____

_____

_____

_____

_____

What do you think are your biggest weaknesses? Why?

_____

_____

_____

_____

_____

How could you rephrase those as strengths?

_____

_____

_____

_____

pay
it
forward

It's so easy to go about your day (or your whole life!) keeping your mind focused on your personal goals and tasks at hand, to stay in your own lane. But one of the most beautiful parts of focusing on a word and knitting it into every aspect of your life is that you begin to see that word everywhere you look. You'll see the *strength* in a friend battling cancer, in how your sister *inspires* at-risk kids, and the *faith* of a work colleague dealing with her divorce with grace. And you'll feel it too. You'll feel the struggle of a recent grad trying to *create* something magical for herself, the *love* of a single mom working as hard as she can to feed her kids, and the *brave* woman experiencing homelessness asking for help or a second chance.

Everywhere you go, these words will call to you, and you won't be able to stop yourself from answering. You'll want to pay it forward, to share the word that's helped you so much with others who may need it. Many people assume that paying it forward is something you do at the end of a focus on your word, when you are ready to let it go and choose a new word. And while you certainly can make a point of doing that, I'd say every word we've discussed here can inspire you to pay it forward from the moment you choose it.

PASS IT ON

Paying it forward is the ripple effect that will change the world. It isn't just about a one-time good deed or donation. Instead, it's about looking outside of ourselves and noticing all of the needs around us every single day. The world can be a hard, sharp-edged place. There are so many injustices, so many people who slip through the cracks and just need a little help to get back up again. Your word can help you find places both big and small where you can help.

Not all of us can do great things. But we can do small things with great love.

—MOTHER TERESA

I believe we have endless opportunities and chances to redeem the broken, homeless, and lost. To show love, dignity, and hope to the hopeless and overlooked. I believe God's heart breaks for every single person who is hurting and needs a word of encouragement. Your word, the one you've chosen to focus on, can be that word for you and for everyone you come into contact with. Use your word, whatever it is, to find ways to help. It's like a compassion homework assignment: to see people who are hurting and pass your word on through your actions to spread even more hope, strength, and love. These words have a magical way of finding kindred souls, like magnets. It's a beautiful thing, and I truly believe it's our collective purpose to speak life and encouragement to one another when we need it most.

YOU'VE GOT WHAT THEY NEED

People may think they don't have enough energy, time, money, or qualifications to "help." Most of the time, you won't feel qualified. You might need training to work for a certain organization, or more education

EVERY WORD MATTERS

if you want to make helping a career by becoming a teacher or social worker. But to intentionally seek kindness and serve a bit? I can promise that you are as qualified as anyone else. If you show up with love, empathy, and compassion, you have what it takes to help.

I'm not suggesting you need to start a nonprofit or give up every Saturday to volunteer. Of course, if you want to do those things, you should! So often when people think of helping others, they think of big things like raising thousands of dollars for a cause, but paying it forward can be something small too. Maybe you see someone who is alone and needs a listening ear, or you know your local food bank is struggling so you donate a few boxes of mac 'n cheese.

Little steps add up over time, and they can often be the start of something bigger. When I saw a hungry couple with nowhere to live, I wasn't thinking about starting a charitable movement; I just wanted to connect with them and offer some love and support, so I started with buying them a simple dinner. Our conversation over steaks gave me the idea to hire people experiencing homelessness, and Rob and Cera became my first two employees. Though I reached out to help them, they ended up helping me in ways I never could have anticipated. Rob

SMALL STEPS TO A BIG IMPACT

Feeling intimidated by the concept of paying it forward? Start small. Here are a few things to get you started!

- On your birthday, set up one of those birthday fundraisers on Facebook or another social media site. Pick an organization you like, and make a plea to friends and family to donate. Helping others is a great way to start a new year!
- Donate to your friends' fundraisers on social media, even if it's only a few dollars. Every penny counts!
- Call a friend out of the blue and check in. You never know what's happening behind closed doors, and it can make someone's day to hear you're thinking of her.
- Send your child's teacher $5 for a cup of good coffee—you know she needs it!

- Make up a few small care packages, and keep them in your car to give to anyone you come across experiencing homelessness. These kits can include a toothbrush, travel toothpaste, travel deodorant, wet wipes, snacks, feminine hygiene products, or even a gift card to a fast-food restaurant.
- Make an easy pasta dinner, and invite a neighbor who lives alone to eat with you.
- Go without your morning latte for a week (you can do it!), and donate that money to a cause you love instead.
- Share a post on social media about a good cause. Even if you can't donate right now, maybe someone you know will.
- Say something kind to everyone you see for a whole day. Everyone loves a compliment, and you never know—that might be the only nice thing someone hears that day!

and Cera then transitioned out of homelessness and moved on to exciting new careers. But, as a result of that one dinner, The Giving Keys has helped transition 130 individuals out of homelessness by providing employment. Big impact from one small step.

FIND YOUR SHINE

Not sure where to start? Well, what lights you up inside? What do you love doing? What are you so good at doing that it's second nature? I want to challenge you to use those things to bring light to others. I naturally want to hear the deep, vulnerable, real stories of everyone I meet. When I see someone who might need an ear to listen, I can't help myself. I go over and introduce myself and start asking questions. Before I know it, I've heard her entire life story and I'm texting a friend to connect her with someone who can offer relief for her specific situation. A lot of people out there are lonely and overlooked. They just want someone to treat them with respect, to listen to them, and to show that they are seen.

If you have great organizational skills, why not offer to help

Pay it Forward

organize volunteers for a charity 10K? Are you good with kids? Offer to help out with childcare during programs for moms at your local church or community center, or offer to babysit for free for a family you know is struggling. A whiz in the kitchen? Volunteer a few hours to do food prep at a soup kitchen or food bank. There's no rule that says you have to do something you aren't comfortable with to help others. This is one area where I believe it's okay to embrace your comfort zone. There are organizations and people out there in need of just about every skill set, so use the skills you've got to make an impact.

UN-BREAK YOUR HEART

When you know what type of thing you'd like to do, you can pick whom to help. If you already have an organization you love or a group of people to help in mind, great! Get to it! But if you aren't sure where to start, I want you to give serious, sincere thought to what breaks your heart. Which issues or injustices have you read about or seen on the news that make your stomach drop? Does the thought of hungry kids unable to get school lunches make your blood boil? Does seeing an elderly man begging on a corner make you tear up? Like me, maybe you hate to think of anyone being lonely, insecure, or ignored. Whatever the issue, that's your place to start.

Be intentional about this. It's easier to push helping others to the bottom of your list. You land a new project at work, you have bills to pay and fires to put out, your kid needs extra TLC or tutoring—and before you know it, your time is all spoken for. If you don't make a point of committing to something, somewhere, somehow and making a difference (even if it's just leaving old books or your lemons from your lemon tree outside for neighbors to take), it gets difficult to squeeze it in later. If your schedule is inconsistent from week to week, that can mean intentionally looking out for and seizing any opportunity that pops up. I invited Rob and Cera to dinner because seeing people with nowhere to live and nothing to eat just kills me. I didn't have cash on me to give them, but I did have my credit card. I was actually supposed to go to an acting class I had already paid for, but I couldn't ignore the tugging in my soul that I was supposed to dive deeper into these people. The thing I could do in that moment was buy them dinner and treat them with respect and dignity.

Be kind, for
everyone
you meet is
fighting a
hard battle.

—PLATO

I'd been touring for months at a time, so I hadn't been able to volunteer anywhere regularly, but deeply connecting with others to better understand the meaning of life was still in the forefront of my mind. It's not the first time I've done something like that, and it won't be the last. Listen to your Peace-O-Meter when you see someone in need. Is it nudging you to action?

Look into your past. Which parts of your story have made you feel defeated, hurt, small, or vulnerable? Each key fits a different lock, and everything you've gone through has shaped the kind of key you are. There is a lock out there just waiting for you to come along, a door that no one else can open. We all have different gifts, different struggles, and different stories. Each of us was made for unlocking and unleashing something meaningful into the world. When you can combine the things you love to do with the injustices that break your heart, you'll find yourself in a whole new type of zone. That's when paying it forward snowballs and makes the biggest impact.

Reflect

I want to leave you with questions to journal about, discuss with a trusted friend, or reflect on as you work to pay it forward.

What are the things in our world that break your heart? These can be injustices, issues, or even a group of people. What about those situations specifically gets to you?

_____

_____

Is there something from your past that makes you more empathetic to those issues than to others?

_____

_____

What are you best at? What do you really enjoy doing?

_____

_____

_____

_____

_____

How can you combine the things you love to
do with the issues that break your heart?

_____

_____

_____

_____

the next word

You'll know when it's time to pick a new word. I always find that toward the end of my time focused on the previous word, a new one starts popping up everywhere I look, as though my old word is pointing the way to the new. I'll never be completely done with this process. Each season of my life brings new challenges, feelings, and circumstances that require a new version of me, and I find myself reaching for words I thought I'd retired. Heck, sometimes I even focus on more than one word at a time. I might need *strength* and *faith* to get through a difficult season. Or maybe I need *love* and *create* to get me out of a slump and onto something new.

When I had *Love Your Flawz* engraved on the very first necklace from The Giving Keys, it was a reminder to be intentional about doing just that. I wanted to rewrite my story of shame, fear, and comparison about my body and life into a story of healing, confidence, and inspiration. I needed that tangible reminder on days when it felt anything but natural to see all of my imperfections as beautiful and lovable instead of shameful secrets to cover up. (If you read my last book, *You Are the Key*, you know what I mean—*wink*.) But over time, being intentional about embracing my flaws made it easier, until I didn't need that daily reminder anymore (at least most days!).

As I chose the words for The Giving Keys, I chose the words I needed for healing, for accepting myself, and for representing who I most want to be. I knew I couldn't be alone in needing them.

Writing these words into my story will be a lifelong journey for me. Some days I won't even have to think about my chosen word, and other days I will need to repeat that word over and over to myself all day long. These words are never-ending, beautiful intentions to strive for. I believe you have the willpower to choose to set aside time for yourself, to meditate on what is good for your mind, body, and soul, and to keep working toward becoming the best version of yourself you can be.

Don't feel discouraged if you need to focus on the same word for a

To stay with that shakiness—
to stay with a broken heart,
with a rumbling stomach, with
the feeling of hopelessness
and wanting to get revenge—
that is the path of true
awakening. Sticking with that
uncertainty, getting the knack
of relaxing in the midst of
chaos, learning not to panic—
this is the spiritual path.

—PEMA CHODRON

while. It's not a failure to need a word longer than someone else does. There's no shame in this game! Shame is so incredibly limiting. Along with fear and comparison, shame is one of the biggest barriers that holds us back. Each of us is on a journey all our own. It won't look like anyone else's when we're finished.

When we see someone up ahead, we tend to feel ashamed that we aren't further along or that we aren't moving as fast as she is. But the truth is that life isn't a race, and we can't possibly know what her journey looks like. You don't know how long she's been on this particular road, or how many miles she's already covered on another road just to get here. You might be sharing the same road for a bit, but it won't be forever.

If we let shame take hold, we may become so focused on where she is that we miss the turnoff to the path that was always meant to be ours. Go at the pace that feels best for you, even if that means you keep the same word for years. And cheer for the women up ahead of you and those coming up behind you. How wonderful is it that life isn't a race with winners and losers? Instead, it's a collection of remarkable journeys that come together to create a beautiful tapestry of healing, redemption, overcoming, perseverance, and love.

No matter what your path is, I'm certain you'll make some wrong turns. You'll wonder if you're getting it "right." You'll question yourself and the people around you. You'll have days when you feel shame, comparison, fear, and guilt. You will definitely feel like a failure sometimes. But I believe you have it within you to work through and release the pain brought on by those feelings.

Remember that pain, failures, and setbacks stretch you. They remind you that you are a fighter. Don't ever quit believing you can heal. Don't ever quit believing you can persevere. Don't ever quit believing you can grow. And don't ever quit believing your journey can (and will!) make a difference. Healing and restoration are there for you to claim. Freedom is there for you to claim. Give yourself grace on your journey of failing and healing because you're enough right now, just as you are.

When you feel ready to let your word go, you'll know. Your word will have taught you everything you needed for this moment, and you'll be ready to move on to something else. You'll hear it and feel it woven into all the parts of your story, ready for you to draw on it again if you need it. You'll feel excited about the challenge of a new word and all it could mean for your career, relationships, goals, and habits. When I pick a new word, I'm always ready to shout it out to the world. It always feels like a fresh start just brimming with possibility.

Look back at all of the questions you've reflected on and answered throughout this book. Do you notice a pattern? Is there a challenge or theme that you've seen emerging around you lately? Is there a word or phrase you just can't seem to get out of your head? Reach out to the people who know you best—do they have a word in mind for you? So often the word we need most chooses us as much as we choose it. Chances are that just answering the questions in this paragraph will have led you to your new word.

Remember, we need all of these words in different seasons of life. So if you are struggling to choose your next focus and nothing is jumping out at you, choose a word that feels like something you want more of in your life, or a word that reminds you of a quality you already have but may forget about sometimes, or even the word that seems like the most fun to you. There is no wrong answer here.

Language provides us with an endless number of words we all crave and need. The idea was never to limit yourself to one list of words (which is why we've always offered a custom word option at The Giving

MORE INSPIRING WORDS

You don't have to choose one of the words in this book. Use what you've learned here, and apply it to one of these other great words! (I love seeing all the personalized custom words people order like these on their Giving Keys!)

- rest
- action
- slow
- enough
- open
- heart

- joy
- peace
- rhythm
- driven
- calm
- forgive

- recover
- heal
- embrace
- search
- breathe
- fight

Keys!). The idea has always been to help people find the key to their own healing and self-love through intentionally embracing words that can help everyone. Your next word may be a different one. Most of the exercises in this book can be used for other words. Once you are in the practice of focusing on a word, it will become second nature to be intentional about weaving it into your life.

Reflect

I want to leave you with questions to journal about, discuss with a trusted friend, or reflect on as you step boldly into what's next.

What is the biggest challenge you have in your life right now? Is there a word you can think of that relates directly to that?

_____

_____

Is there a quality that you feel like you need? Are you feeling anxious and in need of some bravery? Are you feeling weak and in need of strength? Are you feeling grumpy and closed off and in need of love?

_____

_____

Is there something you feel is missing in your life?
Something you've been craving more of? Your next
word may have something to do with that.

_____

_____

_____

Write down every word that pops into your head. Come back
to the list after a good night's sleep, and circle the ones that
feel best to you. Take another break and come back. Is one
of those words jumping out to you? That's your word!

_____

_____

_____

It's important to remember the bigger picture of your story when you find yourself in a season where you feel you need *all* the words, or that maybe every word feels inadequate. Each story is made up of chapters and phrases, storylines that dance around each other to culminate in one thrilling conclusion. Every chapter is important. My hope for you is that this practice of embracing these words can help you turn your failures, imperfections, scars, losses, heartbreaks—and, yes, flaws—into the keys to your own beautiful story of success, discovery, freedom, and love for yourself and others. I hope the words you choose inspire you to see the world with fresh eyes and find your place, your purpose in the bigger tapestry to make the impact you were born to make. I'll be cheering you on the whole way.